PERSONAL STRATEGIES FOR LIVING WITH LESS STRESS

RICHARD A. STEIN, M.D.

John Gallagher Communications Ltd./New York

John P. Gallagher, Sr.

    for
Little things well remembered.

The author, **Richard Alan Stein, M.D.** is Associate Professor, Department of Medicine, Cardiology at the State University of New York and the Director of the Cardiac Exercise Laboratory at Downstate Medical Center in Brooklyn, New York. In addition he is the Director of the Cardiac Intervention and Rehabilitation Program at the 92nd Street Y in New York City and the Acting Director of the Institute for Sports Medicine, Brooklyn College.

Book Design by Susan Tauber
Art Direction by Catherine Snee
Production by Weinglas Typography Co. Inc.

Manufactured in the United States of America.

TABLE OF CONTENTS

The following people, or their work, were helpful in the preparation of this material:

Joan C. Adler
Director of Rehabilitation Laboratory
New York University Medical Center
Goldwater Memorial Hospital
New York, N.Y.

Dr. Charles Berry, M.P.H.
Former Chief Medical Director of the
United States Space Program

Jane E. Brody
Author and Personal Health Columnist
The New York Times
New York, N.Y.

Bernard Brucker, M.D.
Director of the Biofeedback
Laboratories
University of Miami
Miami, Florida

David G. Fournier, Phd
Associate Professor
Department of Family Relations and
Child Development
Oklahoma State University
Stillwater, Oklahoma

Jonathan F. Katz, Phd
Senior Psychologist
New York University Medical Center
Goldwater Memorial Hospital
New York, N.Y.

Hamilton McCubbin, Phd
Professor and Head of the Family
Social Science
University of Minnesota
St. Paul, Minnesota

Brian L.G. Morgan, Phd
Assistant Professor of Nutrition
Institute of Human Nutrition
College of Physicians and Surgeons
Columbia University
New York, N.Y.

Robert J. Paluck, Phd
Director of Behavioral Medicine
International Center for the Disabled
New York, N.Y.

The Surgeon Generals Report on
Health Promotion and Disease
Prevention

PERSONAL STRATEGIES FOR LIVING WITH STRESS and its supporting material are designed to create new self-awareness, particularly with regard to stress. These materials are tools for action in a healthy and effective manner, and for the measurement of your efforts and progress.

For new habits to take root, to be able to sustain themselves effortlessly, requires planning and preparation. Too many of us do not plan when establishing new behavior. This preparation does not involve anything complicated. Thought, patience, confidence, and competence are all that is required—mundane qualities without which most new efforts are made more difficult or fail.

Discouragement is the enemy of efforts to change. Poor planning and careless execution will ensure discouragement and preclude success. Use this book in good health.

Chapter

1 The Impact of Stress

Understanding and Control

What Is Stress?

You could not live without stress. Stress, like pain, begins at birth and remains common to the human condition throughout your life and that of every other human being who ever lived. It is not merely universal, it is endemic and omnipresent. In the functioning of our biological systems, normal stress is necessary and vital: Through variations on the themes of fight or flight, stress reactions mobilize us to adapt to changing stimuli.

Life is constant change and these changes demand an adaptive response. The body cannot survive otherwise. Sometimes these reactions are slight, hardly noticeable. Other times, for example, at a sporting event, we experience briefly intense stress over the possibility of a disappointing outcome. But it is those reactions to acute stress, from the threat

1

of physical harm for example, that are most obvious. In some instances the controlled exposure to stress, let us say a horror movie, is actually pleasurable.

Stress can kill, too. The bad news is that too much stress can be fatal and you may well be unaware of how much is too much. It is now known that the most malign effects of stress can be *deferred* and can accumulate until excessive levels are reached. Compounded stress can contribute to sudden death—as it does each year for thousands of victims of heart attack and stroke; or it can contribute slowly and insidiously— as it does for millions—to a vast assortment of other equally devastating physical and mental disorders. Long periods of stress unfailingly leave their mark.

In other words, if you have a protracted history of stress exposure it is likely to result in some illness, sometime in the future. The good news is that PERSONAL STRATEGIES can help you recognize your exposure and sensitivity to stress— and then to control it.

What can you do about stress? You need not be a helpless victim. Stress is not constant and immutable. There are many kinds and degrees of stress which can be categorized and measured. Your personal program of *stress management* proceeds from a fundamental awareness: As you learn to recognize stress, you can measure the levels and effects of the several kinds of stress that will commonly occur in your life. You then will have the power to alter your response to much of that which is stressful.

Because the symptoms of stress are individualized and dynamic, recognizing them is not always easy; in many instances it will require from you a new sensitivity, a more advanced level of self-awareness. If you understand that you can significantly reduce your stress levels, thereby diminishing the harmful and even fatal consequences of stress, you should be

2

able to cultivate the motivation and make the sustained effort to implement your strategy. *It can save your life.* This book will help you formulate a *personal strategy* for stress reduction.

Stress is a recent medical discovery. Stress has been studied objectively by scientists for less than forty years. In that same period of time, the ramifications of modern technology have contributed new sources of stimuli and stress which were unimaginable when that scientific study began. Because of our changing and expanding world each generation operates at continually higher levels of visual and aural stimulation, both voluntary and involuntary.

Stress may be said to reside in and proceed from a galaxy of environmental influences. Your body's complex machinery of checks and balances responds reflexively to keep you and your system on an even keel. As different demands are made upon us every hour of every day, our hormonal systems make adjustments to those demands, most often going unnoticed.

During periods of stress medical scientists can "see" or measure actual physical and chemical changes: Either the adrenal glands become enlarged or the lymphatic tissues shrink. The shrinkage can be observed by measuring their weight and the productivity of adaptive hormones.

Other changes occurring during a stress period might also include increased production of a hormone called norepinephrine; an increase in heart rate, blood pressure, and respiratory rate; a higher blood-sugar level; enlarged pupils; and even changes in psychogalvanic skin response (PGR) which is an indicator of the body's electrical activity. As you can see, a lot of *unseen* activity goes on during stress.

We are all the same except in the ways in which we are different. Much still needs to be learned about the basic characteristics and the more subtle effects of stress, but this much is certain: When the stress reaction is triggered, the same physiological and chemical processes occur in *everyone*; but among separate individuals there are wide differences in sensitivity to the stimulus and susceptibility to some of the consequences of the stress-reaction process. An event which disables you may merely invigorate someone else. Moreover, your specific sensitivity to stress will likely vary with time and the course of events in your life. Biologically speaking, you're just not the same person you used to be, or will be in the future. It is our *response* to stress that is a major determinant of how damaged we may become. A *stress reaction* occurs immediately and involuntarily; a *stress response* can occur over an extremely long period of time.

Identifying Stress

How to understand the differences between individuals, or within the same individual at different times and how to find the keys to stress management.   We know that stress sustains life. Everything you experience stimulates your body to make adaptations to insure your preservation, your viability against the most diverse aggressions. Without stress, you simply could not survive.

Why is stress so dangerous?   When the stress-reaction mechanism is overloaded, when the hormonal system becomes exhausted through overuse, its malfunction can aggravate your body's health, where the normal function would be to protect your body against the assault of stress. Under continued provocation, stress can adversely affect your immune functions, leaving a healthy body suddenly far more vulnerable to illness, a direct consequence of the weakened capacity to accommodate stress.

4

Stress is a time bomb.   Still more dangerous, the cumulative effects of stress can be delayed for long periods of time. If you have had a history of excessive stress exposure, or have experienced a cluster of intense stress-producing life events, physical evidence of its eroding effect can be measured medically in the decreased amount of adaptive hormones produced by the lymphatic system.

It has long been assumed that physical and mental stress play predisposing and exacerbating roles in some illnesses. Not only has this been established, but medical research now confirms that the body's response to stress can become a critical component of *any* disease. And when the pressure of stress reaches such levels that you truly "can't cope with it," *some illness results.*

Where stress caused the illness.   The following are examples in which stress has been linked to serious illness:

● From a large group of women suspected of having cervical cancer, physicians were able successfully to predict which women would be at higher risk based upon recent stressful life events, especially when compounded by emotional feelings of despair and hopelessness.

● Two thousand people were asked to recount their life changes and medical histories during the preceding ten years, and the episodes of illness were checked against the scores on the life changes report. While those who reported low scores in life changes for a particular year enjoyed good health the following year, *nearly three out of four* with the greatest number and most radical life changes reported severe illness, which tended, moreover, to involve multiple episodes.

● In studies involving thousands of naval personnel, stressful life events that occurred in the six months prior

5

to tours of duty were compared to shipboard medical records compiled during the six-month cruise. Those with the highest number of life changes showed a rate of illness *fifty percent greater* than those with the fewest life changes.

On the other hand, the absence of stress (or its reduction) has been linked to health benefits.

● In research among heart-attack victims, it was established that a reduction in stressful life events led to psychological health and data suggested an improved survival.

In short, stressful life events will contribute to illness, and it would seem *cause* illness. But your *personal strategy* can alter responses to produce a salutary impact, reducing or altogether eliminating the damaging effects which might otherwise ensue from those same stressful life events.

Stressful life events are inescapable. Their capacity to do harm is not.

Who's got a stress-prone personality? Like fingerprints and snowflakes, no two personalities are exactly alike. Contributing to these differences in personality are many factors governing an individual's response to stress. Growing medical evidence points to the relationship between personality types and certain illnesses, suggesting that individuals exhibiting certain personalities are far more likely to contract and suffer from particular diseases than individuals of different personality characteristics.

The long-term study of Dr. Caroline Thomas of the Johns Hopkins Medical Institution has revealed that some combinations of psychological characteristics have been found to have *predictive potential* for the occurrence of specific diseases. For example, evidence of such stress/disease linkage is found in

6

the disease of *asthma*. Studies reveal that asthmatics who are immature, introverted, and incapable of handling stressful situations are far more likely *not* to improve than are asthmatics with sharply differing personality profiles. All this leads to the conclusion that the "asthmatic personality" is not caused by asthma but, rather, the personality itself contributes to the disease.

Stress plays an enormous role in gastrointestinal disorders. If you've suffered from ulcerative colitis, ulcers, anorexia nervosa, vomiting, obesity, constipation, and diarrhea, it is possible that stress had a causal or exacerbating responsibility, and stress might well have prolonged the disorder.

These examples hardly constitute an exhaustive list. Stress has been linked to heart disease and other major disorders such as diabetes, arthritis, multiple sclerosis, several forms of cancer, and—of course—hypertension.

It is clear that to manage stress effectively requires a serious and comprehensive analysis of all the events in your life from which stress emanates.

Take Your Own Inventory

The body of data on stress and its effects is growing steadily. It comes not only from the medical laboratory, but also from long-term statistical studies of thousands of people whose health changes were evaluated against the background of the stressors to which they were exposed by the flow of life's events. *Life Events Research* examines stress as you actually encounter it in the real world.

The process is remarkably uncomplicated, and accessible to the layman. The basic tool of measurement and analysis is a standardized checklist representing common situations arising from personal, family, occupational, financial, and other often-confronted events that require or trigger change in the pattern of your life. Each item is assigned a *stress value* based upon the intensity of the event, the nature of the adjustment necessary to accommodate the change, and the length of time required for the adjustment.

The scientific community first gave recognition to this kind of research at the Conference on Life Stress and Bodily Disease, sponsored by the Association for Research in Nervous and Mental Disease, in 1949; and the Holmes Rahe Social Readjustment Rating Scale (SRRC) was the first instrument to gain widespread acceptance in the measurement of stress in the inventory of life events. The Family Inventory of Life Events and Changes (FILE) and the Personal Reflections on Family Life and Employment Stressors (PROFILES) are more recent tools, and both cast a much broader net for you, measuring stress within your family and the workplace. We will see each of these tools in the next chapter.

It all comes down to you. It is important to emphasize that the causes of excessive stress are not borne on the wind. Surely some inescapable life events—or combinations of events—provide specific kinds and levels of stress. The detailed characteristics of each of these stimuli and your perception of them significantly affect their potential impact on you. Yet every individual has a unique collection of *personal risk factors,* and these are probably more important than anything else mentioned so far in determining whether stress exposure will be harmful. The comforting irony is that many of these critical factors may be controlled because they are *voluntary*: All personal lists of risk factors should include age, heredity, personality type, mental predisposition, diet, exercise, smoking, alcohol and drug abuse. Only the first two are forced upon us involuntarily. The others—albeit in different ways and in varying degrees—may be *controlled* if our lives depend upon it. In some instances, that is precisely the case.

It may be already apparent that limited ability (or inability) to exercise control over these risk factors may result in an adverse response to excessive stress, and can lead to a variety of illnesses. More alarming, however, is the little known fact that the *combined potential for harm from several risk factors* is far greater than merely the sum of their individual potentials. They interact, reinforce, and may even multiply each other.

It is the controllability of any risks—and often the significance of controlling only a *few*—that lies at the heart of your own program for stress management, health promotion, and disease prevention. This comprises your *personal strategy for living with less stress.*

Unmanaged stress is a dangerous business. Doctors and social scientists now recognize that stress is related not only to illness, but that generally it is becoming a growing problem for many millions of people. Up to *half* of all general and corporate medical practice patients are suffering from stress-related problems. Some estimates of the growing impact of stress, measuring the cost of lost work days, hospitalization and outpatient care, diminished creativity, and death, total *ten billion dollars annually*! Successful stress management could reduce that staggering total loss dramatically.

It is already a serious matter for all of us. Now you must look—maybe for the first time but not the last—at your own life for the presence and sources of stress. You may have to unlearn some old notions of stress, and learn a new definition of what constitutes good health for you today and tomorrow. Stress is not an illness, and cannot be treated with bromides and over-the-counter medications. To relieve stress, you must begin with a critical assessment of your whole life. You must start at the beginning, ignoring nothing which might be a place for stress.

Once you have examined the sources of stress in your life, you are going to begin discovering which opportunities are available to *you* for avoiding the more harmful effects.

Finally you are going to create a proper program—a *Personal Strategy*—for yourself to serve your specific needs, to make those changes, no matter how small or modest, changes that will work for a lifetime, a lifetime with less stress.

Chapter

2 The Symbiosis of Stress

Recognizing Stress at Work and in the Home

Quantifying Stress

Stress, on some level, is constantly occurring in your life. It is pervasive and interactive. It can be an unending cycle of cause and effect and cause, a dog frantically chasing its tail. If unmanaged, then frustration, exhaustion, and illness result.

The impact of cumulative life changes upon the health of an individual has been a major concern for more than ten years. However, the concept of cumulative life changes has only recently been applied to *Family Stress.* In this chapter we are going to attempt to determine the potential stress exposure to which you and your family may be subject, and to try and understand some of the sources of those stressors or strains both within and outside of your family by measuring the accumulative number of known life events that make demands on your resources.

Inside your family, for example, the causes could be a financial crisis, illness, a childbearing, or transitional strain. Outside of your family there is a great deal of interaction, particularly in the workplace, some of it stress-producing. Until recently very little was known about how to identify and quantify the extent of the interrelationship for typical families. But now assessment tools have been designed that measure some of those stresses and their impact on your everyday life.

Life is marked by change, much of it welcome. But stress is implicit in change, and change always calls for some measure of readjustment. Although any change in the ongoing pattern of your life is therefore stressful to some degree, some life events are far more stressful, more demanding, than others.

The following are the characteristics of a life event that determine its stress impact on your life:

● the suddenness with which the event occurs, and how prepared you are for it;
● the length of time during which the event occurs;
● the intensity of the event, and the extent to which it changes the usual or normal conditions of your life;
● the newness of the event, in terms of your prior life experiences;
● your *perception* of the event as being stressful.

The first of the inventories or assessment tools created to measure the stress of life events was the Holmes Rahe Social Readjustment Rating Scale (SRRS). It was designed principally to determine how much stress an individual may be undergoing as a result of accumulative life events.

It was an important step in coming to understand the relationship between certain life events and stress-related illnesses. But the two more recent inventories you will use in this book are more ambitious than the SRRS. One focuses on the stress that occurs within your family and how it may affect you and others separately; the other inventory examines the interrelationship of stress in the workplace and in your family. Each inventory provides an opportunity to measure your response with other families who have completed the inventories.

Family Inventory of Life Events

The first instrument is the Family Inventory of Life Events and Changes (FILE), a powerful assessment tool. Using the FILE will enable you to (1) identify some of the major stresses that may be wearing away at your family's ability to cope; (2) generate a new level of awareness of what stresses and hardships you have been struggling with; and (3) look at these demands and determine what effects they have on your family as a unit.

It is no less true for your family as a unit than it is for you individually that a dangerous feature of stress is that it is cumulative and its true impact can be delayed for long periods of time. Family stress, arising from an accumulation of life events and strains, plays a major role in individual and family problems. Therefore, one of our objectives is to demonstrate the value of measuring and evaluating your family's stress levels as a part of a larger effort to determine your family's vulnerability and resiliency.

One characteristic of the physiological systems of your body is their selective resistance to change. They want to conserve or maintain a status quo, a phenomenon called *homeostasis.* This phenomenon is also found in the dynamics of groups such as families. They resist all change, to some degree, because change inherently threatens. Yet families undergo constant and necessary life changes as they grow and mature. These changes make demands for readjustment, and excessive changes or demands can eventually tax the family beyond its ability to make satisfactory adjustments. This produces stress.

We have seen dramatic evidence of the relationship between ordinary life events and illness. Now you can recall times of major readjustment in your own life. They are part of everyone's life—college, marriage, childbirth, illness, or change of employment. Yet, as commonplace as they may be, such transitions can be upsetting and, if they occur in a cluster, distressing. Since your family functions as a total unit, a closed system, the smallest event experienced by one member may trigger other changes within the family unit. Some events such as a divorce may require a major reorganization of the family. But whether readjustments are small or large they all are characterized by a period of uncertainty, anxiety, or a sense of loss. In most instances your family readjusts, reorganizes, consolidates, and adapts within the resources available to it without further complicating demands.

Your family has been, and will be in the future, called upon to change its patterns and bring stability to itself. Individual members of your family will change, and have, over time. We all have our cycles. We grow up and grow old. We all have turning points in our lives and it is hoped that we resolve them in a manner that strengthens us and prepares us to master those crises that may lie ahead.

Your family as a whole has its own life cycle, but by keying on the oldest child in the family, social scientists have divided the family cycle into eight stages: married couple without children; childbearing; preschool age; school age; teenage; launching; middle-aged; and aging family. Much as the individual must respond to changing demands in its development, so does your family experience changes in its life cycle. Again, if the family fails to meet any one of these developmental challenges successfully it can lead to unhappiness, disapproval and difficulty with later family tasks.

Most changes are not extraordinary but normal and expected. Dr. Hamilton McCubbin and Dr. Joan Patterson of the University of Minnesota have added the concept of family *Pile-up* to creating the Family Inventory of Life Events and Changes (FILE). By measuring the number and character of numerous life events and family strains, they believe it can explain why some families are vulnerable to the impact of any single stressor and may lack the ability to recover and adapt to a family crisis. The basic assumption is that if your family's resources are depleted, overtaxed, or exhausted from dealing with other life changes it (and therefore its members) may be unable to make further adjustments. Thus, family life changes and strains are *additive* and may be the silent cause for pushing your family to its limit.

These family demands will include the event that appears to produce some change in the family, those demands associated with the event (resulting financial hardship, for example), and prior tension that remains from unresolved stresses some of which are expected in any family. So it is not just the event you must look at, but also at the Pile-up of events that preceded it and the spreading consequences.

How your family responds to stress in the future is dependent in good measure on the presence of Pile-up. This linkage is predicated on your understanding of your family as a system in terms of the *interconnectedness* of its members. What has been unresolved in your family has been unresolved for every member of your family and can add to the pressure of every new stress for each member and the family as a whole. Change in one part of the system requires readjustment by the whole system.

The Family Inventory of Life Events and Changes (FILE) has nine sections: (1) intra-family strains; (2) marital strains; (3) pregnancy and childbearing strains; (4) finance and business strains; (5) work-family transitions and strains; (6) illness and family care strains; (7) family losses; (8) family transitions in and out; and (9) family legal strains. In turn, each of the sec-

15

tions contains a laundry list of possible stress-inducing events. You will note that some of the events listed seldom occur (such as "a child member dies"); but since such major stress events have an enormous impact, any consideration of family stress could not exclude them.

Alongside of each question a number appears. It is an assigned value that indicates the relative stressfulness of the event or strain, an indication of the relative degree of social readjustment your family will have to make in its usual pattern of life as a result of experiencing the event or strain.

FILE can be completed by any adult family member, but it is our suggestion that FILE be completed separately by each adult member. Then, by scoring the FILE separately, you can determine the number, if any, of discrepancies or differences among the adults in your family. It can be an important feature of the examination because the placement of these differences in the nine groups, and their frequency, can reveal possible areas of miscommunication, or significant differences in stress perceptions. Remember, if some member of your family *thinks* an event or situation is stressful, for them it is. Perception of stress is an acceptance of stress.

On the following pages you will find a *completed* sample FILE worksheet for reference and a blank one at the end of the book for your own personal use.

When you've answered all the questions in each of the nine sections, total up the sum of all the stress sources for those statements to which you answered YES. This is a *gross Pile-up* score. Take your score and compare it to others at the same stage of family development (see Table 1), and determine the *adjusted* score. Remember, your Family Stage is determined by the age of your oldest child.

As you will note, all nine Family Stages have mean scores. This number is the *average stress Pile-up score* for all the families in that Stage who have completed the FILE. However, this is to be regarded only as an *average* score: Your family may score well beyond it and still remain with the "normal" range. In fact, the band for the Moderate category is generous. If the Moderate score for your stage is higher than your family's statistically you are in the Low stress group; and if you scored in excess of the Moderate category, your family is in the High stress group.

Your family score does not necessarily indicate your actual stress reaction or exposure. For some families a score of 300 could be an excessive and crushing stress load, whereas for another family a 700 score may be "business as usual." These scores are relative; they are significant only as they compare with other American families. However, they can be occasions for heightening self-awareness, a re-examination of the possible stress sources and loads in your family and possible remedies if necessary.

TABLE 1

COMPARATIVE NORMS FOR FAMILY PILE-UP OVER THE FAMILY CYCLE

| Family Stage | Mean | Stress Level | | |
		Low	Moderate	High
1. Couple	478	0-210	211-719	720 +
2. Childbearing and				
3. Preschool	530	0-220	221-839	840 +
4. School Age	500	0-265	266-734	735 +
5. Adolescent	545	0-240	241-849	850 +
6. Launching	635	0-320	321-949	950 +
7. Empty Nest	425	0-160	161-689	690 +
8. Retirement	395	0-75	76-699	700 +

FILE Example

FAMILY INVENTORY OF LIFE EVENTS AND CHANGES

Hamilton I. McCubbin   Joan M. Patterson

Purpose

Over their life cycle, all families experience many changes as a result of normal growth and development of members and due to external circumstances. The following list of family life changes can happen in a family at any time. Because family members are connected to each other in some way, a life change for any one member affects all the other persons in the family to some degree.

"FAMILY" means a group of two or more persons living together who are related by blood, marriage or adoption. This includes persons who live with you *and* to whom you have a long term commitment.

Directions

"DID THE CHANGE HAPPEN IN YOUR FAMILY?"

Please read each family life change and decide whether it happened to any member of your family—including you.

● DURING THE LAST YEAR
First, decide if it happened any time during the last 12 months and check the appropriate box.
If the answer is YES, enter the score.

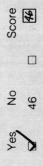

Yes   No   Score

      46 □   46

FAMILY LIFE CHANGES

I. INTRA-FAMILY STRAINS

#	Family Life Change	Yes	No	Score
1.	Increase of husband father's time away from family	✔	46	46
2.	Increase of wife mother's time away from family		51	
3.	A member appears to have emotional problems	✔	58	58
4.	A member appears to depend on alcohol or drugs	✔	66	66
5.	Increase in conflict between husband and wife		53	
6.	Increase in arguments between parent(s) and child(ren)	✔	45	45
7.	Increase in conflict among children in the family		48	
8.	Increased difficulty in managing teenage child(ren)	✔	55	55
9.	Increased difficulty in managing school age child(ren) (6–12 yrs.)		39	
10.	Increased difficulty in managing preschool age child(ren) (2–6 yrs.)		36	
11.	Increased difficulty in managing toddler(s) (1–2 yrs.)		36	
12.	Increased difficulty in managing infant(s) (0–1 yrs.)		35	
13.	Increase in the amount of "outside activities" which the child(ren) are involved in		25	
14.	Increased disagreement about a member's friends or activities		35	
15.	Increase in the number of problems or issues which don't get resolved	✔	43	43
16.	Increase in the number of tasks or chores which don't get done		35	
17.	Increased conflict with in-laws or relatives		40	

II. MARITAL STRAINS

#	Family Life Change	Yes	No	Score
18.	Spouse/parent was separated or divorced		79	
19.	Spouse/parent has an "affair"	✔	68	68
20.	Increased difficulty in resolving issues with a "former" or separated spouse		47	

DID THE CHANGE HAPPEN IN YOUR FAMILY? During Last 12 Mo.

FAMILY LIFE CHANGES

#	FAMILY LIFE CHANGES	Yes	No	Score
21.	Increased difficulty with sexual relationship between husband and wife		58	
III. PREGNANCY AND CHILDBEARING STRAINS				
22.	Spouse had unwanted or difficult pregnancy		45	
23.	An unmarried member became pregnant		65	
24.	A member had an abortion		50	
25.	A member gave birth to or adopted a child		50	
IV. FINANCE AND BUSINESS STRAINS				
26.	Took out a loan or refinanced a loan to cover increased expenses	✓ 29		29
27.	Went on welfare		55	
28.	Change in conditions (economic, political, weather) which hurts the family business		41	
29.	Change in Agriculture Market, Stock Market, or Land Values which hurts family investments and or income		43	

#	FAMILY LIFE CHANGES	Yes	No	Score
43.	Decrease in satisfaction with job/career	✓ 45		45
44.	A member had increased difficulty with people at work	✓ 32		32
45.	A member was promoted at work or given more responsibilities		40	
46.	Family moved to a new home/apartment		43	
47.	A child adolescent member changed to a new school	✓ 24		24
VI. ILLNESS AND FAMILY "CARE" STRAINS				
48.	Parent/spouse became seriously ill or injured		44	
49.	Child became seriously ill or injured		35	
50.	Close relative or friend of the family became seriously ill		44	
51.	A member became physically disabled or chronically ill		73	
52.	Increased difficulty in managing a chronically ill or disabled member		58	

No.	Item		
30.	A member started a new business	[ ] 50	[ ]
31.	Purchased or built a home	[ ] 41	[ ]
32.	A member purchased a car or other major item	[✓] 19	[17]
33.	Increasing financial debts due to over-use of credit cards	[✓] 31	[31]
34.	Increased strain on family "money" for medical/dental expenses	[✓] 23	[23]
35.	Increased strain on family "money" for food, clothing, energy, home care	[ ] 21	[ ]
36.	Increased strain on family "money" for child(ren)'s education	[ ] 22	[ ]
37.	Delay in receiving child support or alimony payments	[ ] 41	[ ]

V. WORK-FAMILY TRANSITIONS AND STRAINS

No.	Item		
38.	A member changed to a new job/career	[ ] 40	[ ]
39.	A member lost or quit a job	[ ] 55	[ ]
40.	A member retired from work	[ ] 48	[ ]
41.	A member started or returned to work	[ ] 41	[ ]
42.	A member stopped working for extended period (e.g., laid off, leave of absence, strike)	[ ] 51	[ ]

No.	Item		
53.	Member or close relative was committed to an institution or nursing home	[ ] 44	[ ]
54.	Increased responsibility to provide direct care or financial help to husband's and/or wife's parent(s)	[✓] 47	[47]
55.	Experienced difficulty in arranging for satisfactory child care	[ ] 40	[ ]

VII. LOSSES

No.	Item		
56.	A parent/spouse died	[ ] 98	[ ]
57.	A child member died	[ ] 99	[ ]
58.	Death of husband's or wife's parent or close relative	[ ] 48	[ ]
59.	Close friend of the family died	[ ] 47	[ ]
60.	Married son or daughter was separated or divorced	[ ] 58	[ ]
61.	A member "broke up" a relationship with a close friend	[ ] 35	[ ]

VIII. TRANSITIONS "IN AND OUT"

No.	Item		
62.	A member was married	[ ] 42	[ ]
63.	Young adult member left home	[ ] 43	[ ]
64.	A young adult member began college (or post high school training)	[ ] 28	[ ]

FAMILY LIFE CHANGES

	DID THE CHANGE HAPPEN IN YOUR FAMILY? During Last 12 Mo.		
	Yes	No	Score
65. A member moved back home or a new person moved into the household	☐	42 ☐	☐
66. A parent/spouse started school (or training program) after being away from school for a long time	☐	38 ☐	☐
IX. FAMILY LEGAL VIOLATIONS			
67. A member went to jail or juvenile detention	☐	68 ☐	☐

FAMILY LIFE CHANGES

	DID THE CHANGE HAPPEN IN YOUR FAMILY? During Last 12 Mo.		
	Yes	No	Score
68. A member was picked up by police or arrested	✔ 57	☐	57
69. Physical or sexual abuse or violence in the home	✔ 75	☐	75
70. A member ran away from home	☐ 61	☐	☐
71. A member dropped out of school or was suspended from school	✔ 38	☐	38
		Total FILE score	861

When you compare this disturbing score with its appropriate Family Stage (5), found in TABLE 1 on page 17, you will see that this family whose oldest child is 15 years old is exposed to a relatively high level of stress. Their concern should be that they do not exhaust their resources and therefore leave the family open to the further consequences of unmanaged stress.

Nevertheless, the pattern that emerges from all these comparative scores does permit us to draw some statistical conclusions.

According to the innovators of FILE, Professors McCubbin and Patterson,

> A high stress family score indicates, usually, that a family has experienced an unusual number of stressors and strains, presumably taxing many of its resources (money, hope, morale, stability, etc.). It is not uncommon for these families to feel out of control, exhausted in the face of high demands. High stress families are considered vulnerable to future stress, prone to experience sudden tension and conflict, seemingly without provocation, and are less able to recover from their impact. Their problem solving abilities may be hampered, leaving them with a feeling that there are many loose ends and unresolved conflicts. While some families under this level of stress may feel comfortable and organized, eventually such excessive demands usually take their toll, particularly if there are insufficient resources to reduce the demands to a more manageable level.

If your family's score fell within the normal range it is considered, on this scale, as nonproblematic. However, families vary greatly in their ability to manage stress. If your family lacks specific resources to cope with stress demands, such as limited access to other sympathetic members of your larger family or professional counseling services, it may struggle at a comparable low level of demand. Even a minor or unexpected event may create a crisis that could bring your family serious problems quite out of proportion with its ability to cope.

If your family score falls into the Low range it would appear that it is unburdened by the demands brought on by changed life events. This is not to say that you are managing your family affairs so it may never experience excessive demands on its resources. On the contrary, self-examination may be called for only to understand how it might cope in the event its score of life events and changes were to be much higher.

Finally, these scores are not intended to be stressful themselves. The scores only suggest areas of Pile-up, potential stress build-up. But if you have scored high it is only prudent that you consider reviewing your family's ability to manage the situation before the family and its individual members suffer.

Personal Reflections on Family Life and Employment

The next assessment tool we will use is the Personal Reflections on Family Life and Employment (PROFILES). Created by David G. Fournier, Ph.D. of Oklahoma State University, PROFILES looks at something social scientists are only now being able to examine closely, though in all likelihood you have experienced it and have always sensed its importance: PROFILES identifies and measures the various ways in which your family and your employment affect each other on a day-to-day basis. Further, it will assess the degree to which your work/family stresses affect your productivity at work and your harmonious relationship at home.

PROFILES covers four basic areas: (1) problems associated with your work; (2) problems associated with your family; (3) impacts or effects associated with your work; and (4) impacts associated with your family. On the computation sheet for your self-scoring (page 32) you will note that under these four basic divisions are sixteen subdivisions, or scales, such as "Work Schedules," "Salary Benefits," "Family Environment," "Work Atmosphere," and "Family Satisfaction."

Looking at your work and family as interactive parts of a larger whole enables you to make a more realistic assessment of work/family stress than treating them as isolated areas. After completing PROFILES, you may be surprised to see the extensiveness of the work/family connection.

PROFILES is a carefully prepared self-evaluation of the relationship between your family and employment and it is hoped that like the earlier assessment, FILE, it will raise your self-awareness about the possible sources of stress and specifically the numerous ways in which your work and family compete for your emotional and physical resources.

On the following pages, you will find a completed sample PROFILES worksheet for reference and a blank one at the end of the book for your own personal use.

Having completed the PROFILES worksheets, the following discussion will outline how you will compare your unique pattern of responses to PROFILES with others who have been involved in its research. Your scores are intended only to help identify personal trends and relative standing to others. They should not be interpreted too strictly and are not meant to imply that situations do not change. In short, the most beneficial use of the self-test on PROFILES is the awareness gained by merely determining the range and extent to which problems between work and family affect your daily living.

Most respondents are surprised to see how many potentially stressful issues frequently occur in a typical week. Your feelings of emotional or physical stress are placed in a better perspective when you objectively determine which of the diverse conflicts and impacts combine to produce this stress. Taken as a whole, conflicts become overwhelming, produce tremendous stress and can even seem incapable of resolution. However, when the contributing stressors are considered individually, as yours will be, and then related to the whole, you can take manageable steps to reduce some of the stresses that make these situations seem overwhelming. PROFILES views

PROFILES Example

INSTRUCTIONS

Please fill in the circles that best describe your experiences.

(Part 1) Please identify how often each of the following events occur in your home life or work setting.

3 = Often   2 = Sometimes   1 = Rarely   0 = Never

(Part 2) When the following situations occur, how much stress or impact does each have on your functioning at home or on the job.

3 = Major Effect   2 = Some Effect   1 = No Effect

Check *DOES NOT APPLY(✓)* if the statement is not possible for you.

WORK AND FAMILY CONFLICT ISSUES

	PART 1 How Often? 3 Often / 2 Sometimes / 1 Rarely / 0 Never	PART 2 Apply Not Apply	How Affected? 3 Major Effect / 2 Some Effect / 1 No Effect
	(fill in one circle) ③ ② ❶ ⓪		(fill in one) ③ ❷ ①
A1 My work schedule creates problems for me	③ ② ❶ ⓪	✓	
B1 Distance to my job creates problems for me	③ ② ❶ ⓪		③ ② ❶

Code	Item								
C1	Getting a promotion is a problem where I work	③	②	①	⓿		③	②	✓
E1	Problems getting along with customers or clients	③	②	✓	⓪		③	②	✓
G1	Children's personal problems need my attention	③	②	✓	⓪		③	②	✓
K1	Anger or tense relations lead to bad work atmosphere	③	②	✓	⓪		③	②	✓
M1	Too tired to do things with family when get home	③	②	✓	⓪		③	②	✓
N1	Scheduling adequate child care is difficult	③	②	①	✓		③	②	✓
P1	Family does not support or approve of job	③	②	✓	⓪		③	②	①
B2	Problems due to changing job site or location	③	②	✓	⓪		③	②	✓
D1	Work conditions are uncomfortable or distracting	③	②	✓	⓪		③	②	✓
F1	My job is not everything I wanted it to be	③	②	✓	⓪		③	②	✓
H1	Marital difficulties are a source of concern	③	②	✓	⓪		③	②	✓
I1	Problems with family financial matters	③	②	✓	⓪		③	②	✓
J1	Too tired or not physically ready when go to work	③	②	✓	⓪		③	②	✓
M2	Nervous, tense or frustrated when get home	③	②	✓	⓪		③	②	✓
O1	Family is neglected and not as close as it could be	③	②	✓	⓪		③	②	✓
A2	Long working hours are a problem for me	③	②	✓	⓪		③	②	✓

WORK AND FAMILY CONFLICT ISSUES

		PART 1 How Often? (fill in one circle) Often 3, Sometimes 2, Rarely 1, Never 0	Apply Not Apply	PART 2 How Affected? (fill in one) Major Effect 3, Some Effect 2, No Effect 1
C2	Employer policy on payment of wages creates problems	③ ② ① ⓪	✓	③ ② ①
F2	My employer demands too much from my job	③ ② ① ⓪		③ ② ①
H2	Problems with parent-child relationships	③ ② ① ⓪		③ ② ①
J2	Loss of time at work because of other problems	③ ② ① ⓪		③ ② ①
M3	My personal health is a problem	③ ② ① ⓪		③ ② ①
O2	Hard to find enough time to be alone with spouse	③ ② ① ⓪		③ ② ①
B3	The place I work is in a dangerous location	③ ② ① ⓪		③ ② ①
E2	Trouble getting along with my employer	③ ② ① ⓪		③ ② ①
G2	My spouses' personality creates problems	③ ② ① ⓪		③ ② ①
J3	Personal concerns reduce my productivity at work	③ ② ① ⓪		③ ② ①

Code	Statement		
M4	My health and satisfaction are affected by problems	3 2 ① ⓪	3 ② ✓
P2	Family disagreements about things related to work	3 2 ① ⓪	3 ② ✓
C3	Salary and benefits of my job creates problems	3 2 ① ⓪	3 ② ✓
F3	Some things about my job are a problem for me	3 2 ① ⓪	3 ② ✓
I2	Lack resources to meet family's desired lifestyle	3 2 ① ⓪	3 ② ✓
L1	Home duties are unfinished or not done very well	3 ② ① ⓪	3 ② ✓
O3	Family members are irritable or tense at home	3 2 ① ⓪	3 ② ✓
C4	My pay is unfair or not enough	3 2 ① ✓	3 ② ✓
F4	Type of job I have creates problems for me	3 2 ① ⓪	3 ② ✓
I3	My lifestyle and personal interests lead to problems	3 2 ① ⓪	3 ② ✓
N2	Family needs and activities are hard to schedule	3 2 ① ⓪	3 ② ✓
A3	Can never be sure what hours I will work	3 2 ① ✓	3 ② ✓
E3	Trouble getting along with some of my co-workers	3 2 ① ⓪	3 ② ✓
I4	Difficulties caused by friends or relatives	3 2 ① ✓	3 ② ✓
M5	Feel guilty about neglect of family	3 2 ① ✓	3 ② ✓
A4	Having no control over work hours is a problem	3 2 ① ✓	3 ② ✓
D2	Work situation is dangerous or unsafe	3 2 ① ✓	3 ② ✓
G3	My personality or personal habits create problems	3 2 ① ✓	3 ② ✓

WORK AND FAMILY CONFLICT ISSUES

		PART 1				Apply Not Apply	PART 2	
		How Often?					How Affected?	
		Often ③	Sometimes ③	Rarely ③	Never ⓪		Major Effect ③ Some Effect ③ No Effect	
		(fill in one circle) ③ ② ① ⓪				✓	(fill in one) ③ ② ①	
J4	Other commitments interfere with my work performance	③ ② ① ⓪					③ ② ①	
L2	Not taking time to do extra things around house	③ ② ① ⓪					③ ② ①	
P3	Disagree on whether should be at work or with family	③ ② ① ⓪					③ ② ①	
C5	My employee benefits are not enough for my needs	③ ② ① ⓪					③ ② ①	
G4	Family member personal problems create difficulties	③ ② ① ⓪					③ ② ①	
J5	Problems concentrating on my job when at work	③ ② ① ⓪					③ ② ①	
N3	Community or school meetings are hard to attend	③ ② ① ⓪					③ ② ①	
P4	Disagree with spouse on need for both of us to work	③ ② ① ⓪					③ ② ①	
F5	My job is demanding, tedious and/or too tense	③ ② ① ⓪					③ ② ①	
K2	Not interested in or happy about my job	③ ② ① ⓪					③ ② ①	

Item			Response
O4	Family satisfaction is less due to other problems	③ ② ① ⓪	③ ②
E4	Problems getting along with some people at work	③ ② ① ⓪	③ ②
I5	Problems created by trying to schedule family needs	③ ② ① ⓪	③ ②
P5	Concern about what spouse does while at their job	③ ② ① ⓪	③ ②
D3	Working conditions at my job are a problem	③ ② ① ⓪	③ ②
H3	Marriage or family matters create problems for me	③ ② ① ⓪	③ ②
N4	Family health checkups or exercise hard to set up	③ ② ① ⓪	③ ①
B4	My job is located in an undesirable place	③ ② ① ⓪	③ ②
H4	Family problems are a source of concern	③ ② ① ⓪	③ ②
K3	Trouble with co-workers causes bad work situation	③ ② ① ⓪	③ ②
L3	Hard to complete household duties when tired or busy	③ ② ① ⓪	③ ①
E5	Supervisor on my job creates problems for me	③ ② ① ⓪	③ ②
N5	Difficult to schedule recreational activities	③ ② ① ⓪	③ ①
H5	Concern about children fighting with each other	③ ② ① ⓪	③ ②
B5	Location of my job leads to certain problems	③ ② ① ⓪	③ ②

© 1981 D.G. Fournier   Oklahoma State University   Stillwater, Oklahoma 74078   All Rights Reserved

Example COMPUTATION OF SCALE SCORES FROM THE PROFILES INVENTORY

Part 1 = How Often
Part 2 = Effect

PROFILES Scale Titles	Addition of Items in Each Scale (Part 1 / Part 2)	Raw Score Totals	Divided By # of Items	Average Scores	Combined Conflict And Impact Score (Graph These Scores) Conflict / Impact / Combined

PROBLEMS ASSOCIATED WITH WORK

Scale	Addition of Items	Raw Score	Divided By / Average	Combined
Work Schedules — Scale A	A1 [1:2] + A2 [1:1] + A3 [1:1] + A4 [0:1] + A5 [0:1]	= A [2:5]	÷ 4 = [.5:1.2]	.6
Job Location — Scale B	B1 [1:1] + B2 [1:1] + B3 [1:1] + B4 [0:1] + B5 [1:1]	= B [4:6]	÷ 5 = [.8:1.]	.8
Salary & Benefits — Scale C	C1 [1:1] + C2 [0:1] + C3 [1:1] + C4 [0:1] + C5 [1:1]	= C [3:5]	÷ 5 = [.6:1.]	.6
Work Environment — Scale D	D1 [1:1] + D2 [0:1] + D3 [1:1] + D4 +	= D [2:3]	÷ 3 = [.7:1.]	.7
Work Relationships — Scale E	E1 [1:1] + E2 [1:1] + E3 [1:1] + E4 [1:1] + E5 [1:1]	= E [5:5]	÷ 5 = [1.:1.]	1.
Job Characteristics — Scale F	F1 [1:1] + F2 [1:1] + F3 [1:1] + F4 [1:1] + F5 [1:1]	= F [5:5]	÷ 5 = [1.:1.]	1.

PROBLEMS ASSOCIATED WITH FAMILY

Scale	Addition of Items	Raw Score	Divided By / Average	Combined
Personal Problems — Scale G	G1 [1:1] + G2 [0:1] + G3 [1:1] + G4 [1:1] + G5 [1:1]	= G [3:4]	÷ 4 = [.8:1.]	.8
Interpersonal Problems — Scale H	H1 [1:1] + H2 [2:2] + H3 [1:1] + H4 [1:1] + H5 [1:1]	= H [6:6]	÷ 5 = [1.2:1.2]	1.4
Family Environment — Scale I	I1 [1:1] + I2 [1:1] + I3 [1:1] + I4 [1:1] + I5 [1:1]	= I [5:5]	÷ 5 = [1.:1.]	1.

IMPACTS ASSOCIATED WITH WORK

Scale	Addition of Items	Raw Score	Divided By / Average	Combined
Work Productivity — Scale J	J1 [1:1] + J2 [0:1] + J3 [1:1] + J4 [1:1] + J5 [1:1]	= J [4:5]	÷ 5 = [.8:1.]	.8
Work Atmosphere — Scale K	K1 [1:1] + K2 [1:1] + K3 [1:1]	= K [3:3]	÷ 3 = [1.:1.]	1.

IMPACTS ASSOCIATED WITH FAMILY

Household Functioning
L1 [2.1] + L2 [2.2] + L3 [2.2] = L [6.5] 3 = [2.17] 3.4

Personal Well-Being
Scale M
M1 [1.1] + M2 [1.1] + M3 [0.1] + M4 [1.1] + M5 [1.1] = M [4.5] 5 = [.81] .8

Family Schedules
Scale N
N1 [0.1] + N2 [1.1] + N3 [1.1] + N4 [2.2] + N5 [2.2] = N [6.7] 5 = [12.14] 1.7

Family Satisfaction
Scale O
O1 [1.1] + O2 [2.1] + O3 [1.1] + O4 [1.1] = O [5.4] ÷ 4 = [13.1] 1.3

Family Consensus
Scale P
P1 [1.2] + P2 [1.1] + P3 [1.1] + P4 [1.1] + P5 [1.1] = P [6.6] 5 = [1.12] 1.2

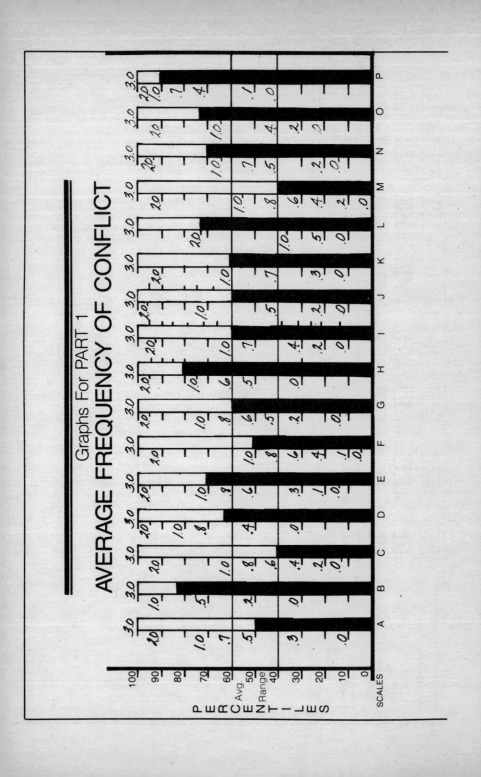

Graphs For PART 1
AVERAGE FREQUENCY OF CONFLICT

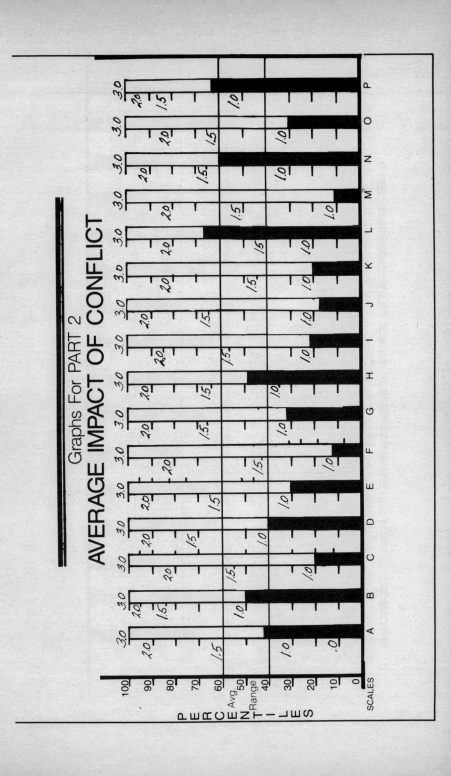

Graphs For PART 2
AVERAGE IMPACT OF CONFLICT

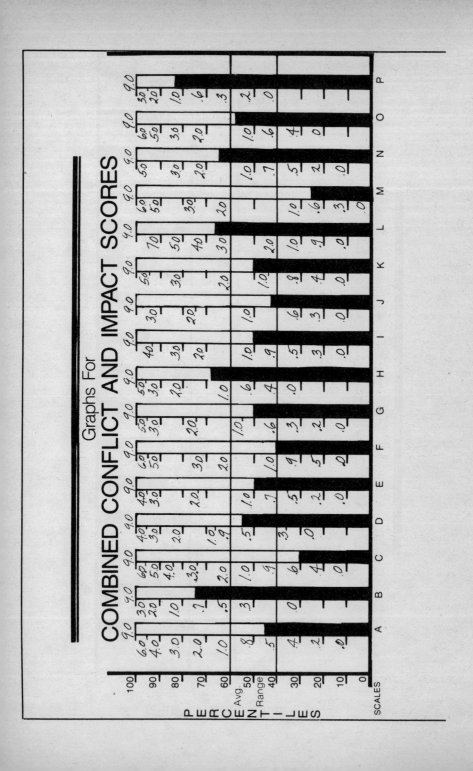

Graphs For
COMBINED CONFLICT AND IMPACT SCORES

conflicts associated with everyday work and family life as part of the same environmental situation and as important factors to consider when you assess your potential for stressful overload.

Aside from gaining awareness about work/family conflicts, the scoring procedure will help you determine how your responses compare with existing norms, or the scores of those other families who have completed PROFILES. You will calculate your score and then simply convert it to a percentile.

For example, your identified conflicts associated with your "Work Schedule" will be charted on a percentile bar graph and there you will see how you related to the norm. A percentile of 85 (determined by reading the percentile column on the extreme left of the graph) would mean that eighty-five out of one hundred persons tested would have less conflict than you while only 15% would have more conflict. On the bar graph those with scores below yours have less and those above have more. Numerous scores over the 70th percentile would indicate considerable work/family conflict and may suggest avenues for resolving some of the stress associated with the situation.

The individual conflict scores are calculated to reflect their average frequency, their average impact, and their combined scores which is an adjustment of the amount of conflict and associated impact per scale or division. This procedure is not difficult. And once you produce your own graph it provides a visual representation of those areas which seem to be most and least conflicting for you. In addition, the graphed scores are averages that permit you to compare these numbers directly with those in your other scales, or divisions.

The scores for this calculation procedure are taken from the sample PROFILE.

Referring to the PROFILES worksheets you completed, note that each of the sixteen subscales in PROFILES is assigned a letter (on the extreme left) from A to P and contains from three to five items. In the example shown, Scale A ("Work Schedule") has four items in various locations within PROFILES. Each of the items has a box divided into two parts: Part 1 for "How Often" each conflict situation occurs and Part 2 for "How Affected." To begin the calculation process, simply find each item in the PROFILES Inventory (A1, A2, A3, and A4) and write in the number of your response to both Part 1 and Part 2 (0, 1, 2 or 3) in the computation tables that follow. Next, add the numbers in Part 1 for all items and put the sum in the box for Raw Scores Totals. Repeat for Part 2. To obtain an average Conflict and Impact Score per Scale, divide the Raw Scores individually by the number of items (4) and put that result in the proper boxes. Finally, multiply the Average Conflict times the Average Impact (.5 × 1.25) for the Combined Conflict/Impact Score. These scores can be recorded onto the provided graphs to illustrate your relative standing.

Work Schedules
Scale A

	Part 1	Part 2						
A1	1	2	+ A2	7 1	+ A3	0 1	+ A4	0 1	=

	Part 1	Part 2		Conflict	Impact	Combined
				(Graph These Scores)		
A	2	5	÷ 4 =	.5	1.2	.6

Please remember that these scores are experimental in nature and should not be regarded as more than a tool for a self-assessment and awareness. In the chapters that follow, you will learn about strategies for helping to better understand and mitigate the impact of stress in your own and your family's lives.

Chapter
3 Stress Risk Awareness

How You Can Make Personal Measurements

On the Look-Out for Stress

Life abounds with stress. While we may limit our exposure to some stressful events, we do not really change the events themselves, as we have already seen. But the risk of damage or disease arising from stress and from particularly stressful events is seriously increased by individual risk factors.

Some risk factors are unavoidable, beyond your control, and can only be prepared for. Physicians refer to them as *unmodifiable* risk factors. Your age and hereditary history, for example, cannot be altered. They place you in a risk category that is inevitable. Therefore if members of your family have had a heart attack under the age of fifty, or you have diabetes, or you are a male, or you are over the age of forty, your chances of a coronary are inevitably greater than those of

39

someone who shares none of the above risk factors. While you cannot control or avoid these risks, you can influence their pernicious effects through better overall health and by reducing those modifiable risk factors that aggravate the unmodifiable risk factors.

Heightened awareness is the key to what your exposure will be to all of your personal risk factors, especially those which can be moderated or eliminated. Awareness lies at the heart of every successful strategy or effort to reduce stress, but remember: No matter what stress-management program you find or create for yourself, the presence or absence of a sustained commitment fueled by self-interest will determine in the long run whether you produce the kind of results you want and need.

A measure of appropriate self-awareness is your willingness to exercise whatever control possible over those modifiable risk factors in your life, such as excessive weight, smoking, lack of appropriate exercise, or alcohol abuse. According to the American Heart Association you are more likely to develop coronary artery disease if:

● you have high blood pressure;
● you smoke cigarettes;
● you have a high level of cholesterol in your blood;
● you are overweight;
● you have a lot of unmanaged stress and tension in your life.

As we have seen, perhaps the most powerful characteristic of risk factors is that in combination they pose a far greater threat to you than as separate risk factors. For example, a smoker with a high cholesterol level and no exercise program may be said to have multiple risk factors. Multiple risk factors have a progressive, synergistic effect. Their sum is greater than their parts. The smoker with a three to five times greater risk of a heart attack, and with a cholesterol level above 275 mg./dl.—which also creates a three to five times greater risk—actually has a fourteen to sixteen times greater risk of a heart attack. Therefore, if you can begin to control the controllable risks you can earn further dividends by avoiding the multiplier effect of several risk factors, even when one or more of those risks is unmodifiable.

The following is a general list of common physical and psychological risk factors. Some of them are or may appear to be unmodifiable and therefore to be tolerated. However, by making your own list you'll see both how many are not necessarily beyond your influence and also how certain elements of your life-style become potentially even more threatening *in combination*. These lists are by no means exhaustive. Keep in mind that the psychological risk factors may seem less specific than the physical risk factors, but they are equally important.

Physical Risk Factors

- Age
- Genetic/Hereditary History
- General Health
- Diet
- Obesity
- Exercise (or lack of exercise)
- Smoking
- Alcohol and/or substance abuse

Psychological Risk Factors

- Personality Type A
- Emotional Sensitivity and Capacity for Depression
- Capacity for Planning and Decision Making
- Attitude Towards the Future
- Defense Mechanisms
- Suppression of Emotions
- Lack of Meaningful Activity

Smoking: A Modifiable Risk Factor

Let's take one physical risk factor and look at it in detail. Of the Physical Risk Factors the one that is clearly voluntary yet may be the most harmful is smoking: It is simply the largest *preventable* cause of illness and premature death in the United States. The statistical evidence on the damaging effects of this habit is staggering:

- Smoking contributes to 25% of all deaths from cancer, and 48% of all male deaths from cancer.
- Cigarette smokers are two or three times more likely to have a heart attack than are nonsmokers.
- Those who smoke one pack of cigarettes daily have a 50% greater frequency/duration of hospitalization than those who do not smoke.
- Those who smoke thirty cigarettes daily are exposed to the equivalent amount of alpha-radiation as someone who has had three hundred X rays in a year.
- People who smoke two packs each day have twice the rate of work absenteeism of nonsmokers.

The damage is not restricted to the smoker. Studies have shown that the infants of smoking parents have nearly twice the risk of being hospitalized with pneumonia or bronchitis, and a study in Detroit indicated that schoolchildren exposed to tobacco smoke at home have twice the expected number of respiratory infections.

Heart disease is the number one cause of death for those over the age of forty-five by a dramatic margin, and remains the principal cause of death for the total population. Yet, not only does your risk of a heart attack increase if you smoke, but it increases with each cigarette and may be more than ten times greater for smokers of twenty-five cigarettes a day when compared to nonsmokers.

Cigarette smoking damages your circulatory system by:

● Stimulating your heart, narrowing your blood vessels, and making your heart beat faster;
● Causing carbon monoxide to be absorbed in the blood in your lungs, replacing oxygen which decreases the supply of oxygen that gets to your heart, makes breathing more difficult, and increases the strain on your heart;
● Making your blood more likely to clot and less able to dissolve clots;
● Causing "extra" heartbeats, which are irregularities that can be seen on your EKG.

A large portion of the smoker's excess risk for heart disease disappears within two years after quitting. Within ten to fifteen years, an ex-smoker's chance of early death from heart disease is no greater than that of someone who never smoked. In fact, if all Americans stopped smoking, coronary death could be reduced by approximately 30%, with a savings of more than two hundred thousand lives every year. Some ten million Americans currently suffer from debilitating chronic diseases caused by smoking.

The dividends for quitting smoking are immediate. Within seventy-two hours the nicotine that was stimulating your adrenal glands and consequently elevating your heart beat is no longer present. As a result there is less strain on your heart. Your heart and lungs begin to function better, and if you have angina its discomfort comes less often. Needless to say, improved breathing and an improved attitude generally encourage greater physical activity, which begins to favorably influence most other risk factors.

There are many examples of the benefit or value of direct action regarding the promotion of health, but a very dramatic instance of a multiple-risk-factor intervention that produced truly promising results is the Stanford Heart Disease Prevention Program, funded by the National Heart, Lung, and Blood Institute. The Stanford Program, begun in 1972, has been monitoring the rates of cigarette smoking, serum cholesterol levels, and uncontrolled hypertension in three Northern California communities. Two of the three employed active risk-reduction activities, including messages designed for television, radio, newspapers, and other media. In one of these two communities, face-to-face counseling also was provided for a sample of high-risk individuals.

Within a two-year period in the two experimental communities, overall heart disease risk fell by about 25% and this included a net reduction of serum cholesterol and a 6% lowering of systolic blood pressures. However, in the community without an active information program, overall risk for heart disease actually increased during the first two years of the study.

The results of this study suggest that without direct intervention (either self-generated or with the help of others) those of us with unnecessarily high risk factors will be at high risk suffering the consequences. Yet as inescapable as the consequences may seem, the actual risk, in many instances, remains avoidable, such as smoking.

Yet despite conclusive and still-accumulating evidence of the link between smoking and stress-related illnesses, smoking is on the rise among women. If current trends continue, medical experts predict that lung cancer will surpass breast cancer as the leading cause of cancer mortality for women by the end of 1984.

Alcohol Abuse: Warning Signs and Coping Strategies

The relationship of stress to many physical risk factors is that, ironically, stress can get you coming and going: Initially stress is often the precipitating cause and later the result of the risk factor. This is often true of alcohol abuse. Many people seek alcohol for relief from stress or its symptoms such as tension or anxiety, but through abuse it eventually not only increases but becomes the cause of new sources of stress. The nature of many addictions is that the substance involved produces the necessary symptoms for the perpetuation of its abuse.

Few people, excepting the very young, need to be educated as to the harmful effects of alcohol abuse. But why so many people continue to abuse themselves with alcohol remains a mystery rooted deeply in the individual problems most people have living their lives. Namely, remove all of life's difficulties and there would probably not be "reasons" to escape from its realities.

That alcoholism continues to be such a widespread medical and social problem can be attributed in part to certain misconceptions that many people cling to, namely that it is a disease that cannot be cured or that it is not a problem requiring treatment. Most people who are not problem drinkers are aware of the warning signals or antecedent cues that indicate a problem, particularly in others. To the problem drinker, even the most self-evident of these cues often lacks the power to convince, if for no other reason than they don't want to be convinced. In looking at our lives, the observations we make are apt to be seen in isolation. The weight of their numbers can, taken in the aggregate, make for a powerful argument. Often, however, we find that we can conveniently reject the ultimate significance of the sum total if we deal with the parts.

Therefore, a diary or personal journal can play a major role in gathering the isolated, the seemingly insignificant or irrelevant experiences or thoughts for consideration at a chosen moment. You may elect to keep a journal in any fashion you find suitable and easiest. The only rule is that you record honestly; it is, after all, for your eyes only.

The problem of any abuse, but particularly alcohol, is both

gross and subtle. It doesn't initially yield to easy identification, as the following sample of journal entries suggests:

- "When I am criticized in the office, I feel like I did when disapproved by my father and the urge to have a drink becomes mandatory."
- "I become annoyed if taken to a restaurant for lunch where I cannot get a (my) drink. I usually will suggest another place and even pay for it."
- "I have failed at stopping my drinking in the past. In fact I am convinced it is impossible for me."
- "If I haven't had a drink I find new business/social situations difficult. I don't feel I am as outgoing and as interesting with others."
- "A drink is always a celebration and reward. At the end of any workday, particularly a trying one, I consider the 'happy hour' my privilege, an entitlement."
- "The only way I can get relief from real tension is to have at least one drink. Possibly two."

The purpose of creating entries of actual drinking episodes, or reflecting on occasions when alcohol plays a key role, is to learn what the cues are in your life that can lead to an understanding of your unique pattern of dependence. The way in which these cues become linked to your compulsive urge to drink is crucial to your designing a program that begins to deal with the problem that has emerged.

Numerous psychological experiments on antecedent cues bear out what most of us have always suspected about stress in certain situations. Threat and criticism drive heavy drinkers to drink more, often without a conscious decision to do so.

As is abundantly clear, the potential or experienced problem drinker faces a problem for which there is no easy or universally successful solution. Broadly speaking there are two ways of helping the problem drinker to regain control. One is to make sobriety more interesting and rewarding. Of course when sobriety is sufficiently distanced it is difficult to speak convincingly of its appeal. And that is further complicated when the craving is experienced against a background of boredom, loneliness, or some other omnipresent problem. However, the support of others is indispensable, particularly when dealing with the problems that bring on the dependency and also the selling of sobriety. The best-known and most effective of the self-help groups counseling alcoholics is Alcoholics Anonymous. But if a group strikes the problem drinker as "unnecessary" or "disturbing," family and friends can be a welcomed resource, surprisingly so. The key ingredient for success in both instances is the honest willingness to stay sober.

The second aid to a problem drinker trying to stop is to rehearse different ways of coping with craving. Again, it is the support of others that often is required to sustain the change and help the problem drinker to remain beyond the reach of the compulsion. Again, the diary which recorded antecedent cues can be of inestimable benefit in determining and inculcating learned coping strategies.

Coping strategies for the problem drinker are only as effective as they are appropriate: In other words, each drinker must design his or her own. The following are samples that suggest the thought process by which a drinker, having recognized that his abuse of alcohol is a potential peril to his health as a personal risk factor, can go about planning a solution. The same kind of empirical approach can be applied to other modifiable risk factors.

In a drinking situation you must be able to anticipate the source and character of those *pressures* that cause you to drink or drink heavily in the first place. Then you must have a prepared series of *strategies*—prepared responses—that allow you to quietly cope with the pressure. Therefore, after carefully consulting your diary or journal and analyzing it for the picture it creates of circumstances that provoke problem drinking, identify the high-risk situations and why they occur. For example, it may be the obligatory professional business lunch or routine stop on the way home with your car pool group. The first thing you may realize is that you are indeed subject to considerable peer pressure to have a drink and therefore their open lack of support for your new commitment is a genuine stumbling block.

The first strategy may be simply to *break the routine*, without an explanation. But if that is not possible or is unacceptable for other reasons, you could attempt to enlist them in your effort. Tell them what your plan is and convince them of your sincerity. If it appears to cause them some discomfort, remind yourself that your wish to make a change is more important than their discomfort. And their disapproval may reflect their own dis-ease with drinking. If at all times you believe in *the primacy of your new priorities* your coping strategies will be seen only as a means to an end. They signify nothing more, to you or anyone else. They are there only to get you where you want to go.

The following strategies might apply in most social situations:

- Never stay so long that you begin to review the merits of having a drink.
- Remember the occasion when you stayed sober and the pleasure of having successfully resisted the impulses or drink signals.
- Have nonalcoholic drinks that do not draw attention to your commitment.
- Learn how to say no firmly to the offer of a drink without an explanation; the explanation may become a topic of discussion you may not want to have.
- When a craving becomes intense get up and leave. It need not be obvious. Leave for the restroom or make a

telephone call. But if necessary leave the room or go home. Remember, you have a new agenda, new priorities that you believe in.

● Never question the value of your commitment when being "forced to drink." Do that later while still sober.

Perhaps the greatest reason most people fail to achieve the results they desire when it comes to planned change is due to *learned helplessness.* They are persuaded that what their past failures indicate is that they cannot do whatever it was they wanted to accomplish. In truth those "failures" probably reflect only their poor preparation and planning. Their chances of success were marginal because of their limited understanding of what any process of change requires.

The reasons people fail to make the changes they desire are probably as numerous as the people who seek planned change. But studies reveal that one of the features common to those who are successful is their use of a *variety* of coping techniques. Addiction Research Units have learned that simple distraction or avoidance of the disapproved behavior (e.g., smoking, binge-eating, alcohol) usually does not prove in the long or short term to be effective. "Survivors" (those who did not suffer a relapse) were found to use something like a thought-stopping technique (page 75) when distraction failed. Therefore, you have to assume that the successful strategy usually must exploit a combination of techniques because all of your personal circumstances are not going to conform to any one coping technique.

Your need to be aware of negative attitudes when attempting change with one or more of your physical risk factors. You must first learn to believe that you can control the situations that trigger your compulsion. That belief must first dismiss most past failures as meaningless; at the same time, those past failures must be examined for the clues they hold as to why the experiment failed.

You must also learn to believe in your ability to master the techniques. Allow your confidence to grow through modest successes, results of efforts that you can be almost assured of achieving.

Your initial efforts need not succeed at first. As a new airplane must be tested, and new products offered on a thirty-day trial basis, so too should your new behavior be tested. A successful test is not necessarily error-free; its success is measured by its ability to eliminate the errors it uncovers so that it will work error-free when used in earnest.

Be patient, start cautiously. Keep your program simple, and within a time frame you can believe. You will be surprised at the change that you will experience regarding renewed and heightened expectations. The first result you should look for and encourage is personal confidence; it is more likely to be a fragile green shoot than a flowering mature plant. Success with problems growing out of a physical risk factor can be attributed finally to a number of sources, but the success you want is that which is self-attributed. If you believe that your results are due primarily or exclusively to external sources, such as tranquilizers, your self-esteem will suffer and under stress a relapse is very likely.

Overweight: A Risk Factor Multiplier

Overweight contributes to the unsuccessful management of stress in so many ways, both psychologically and physiologically. If you weigh too much, an additional work load is placed on your heart. For every pound of fat on your body, your heart has to pump blood through an extra three-quarters of a mile of blood vessels. And it does this about seventy times a minute, unless you have an unusually high pulse rate which means more stress. Even when resting, your overweight body works harder to breathe and needs more oxygen.

Excess weight increases the risk of a number of stress-related illnesses, particularly coronary-artery disease. The heart-attack rate for people who are thirty pounds overweight is twice that for people with normal weight. Statistically, an extra thirty pounds may decrease your life expectancy by four years. And as your weight goes up, so goes your risk. Finally, if you suffer a heart attack your chances for a successful recovery will be adversely affected by the very weight that may have contributed to the coronary.

Two other problems directly affected by excessive weight are hypertension and diabetes. Overweight people are three times as likely to have hypertension and four times as likely to have diabetes. The benefits of losing excess weight is already a subject of daily discourse on television, radio, in newspapers and magazines, perhaps even in your physician's office and among friends and family. The only note that should be added is that if you are over forty years of age not only will your excess weight grow more difficult to lose through the years but it will grow more dangerous. If you are obese it is likely that you will increase your risks of arterial disease and if the disease already exists, your symptoms will increase.

Probably the most critical barometer of any of your stress-related physical risk factors is your blood pressure. Occasional brief periods of increased blood pressure is not usually a problem. But if your pressure is constantly higher than it should be (140/90 or more) it is a serious problem. This is *hypertension*.

Blood pressure is the force exerted by the flow of blood against the artery walls. This pressure reaches a peak with each heartbeat (systole) and then decreases between beats (diastole). When you measure your blood pressure there are two important readings to take: systolic (the larger number) and the diastolic (the smaller number). Normal blood pressure readings should most often be approximately 120/80. If your blood pressure goes up to or beyond 140/90 (and remains there) chances are you have hypertension.

Hypertension is very serious disease for two reasons. First, there are no obvious signs that you have it. It does not mean that you are visibly tense. If you have hypertension and you do not check your blood pressure on a regular basis, initially anyway, you may not become aware of it until its late stages when often it's too late.

Furthermore, if you've had it for a while, your heart must pump harder. Your heart therefore enlarges, and eventually, under this extra burden, it weakens, loses efficiency, and pumps less blood with each beat. Artery walls are injured, clog and eventually choke off blood to the heart, brain, or kidneys, leading to heart attack, stroke or kidney failure. Therefore, it is important you monitor your blood pressure systematically, over a fixed period of time. This procedure should be supervised by your physician, if only to assure that your results are reliable and can be properly interpreted.

If you do have high blood pressure what do you do? No matter what your age or gender the following advice applies. Blood pressure appears to rise with age for most Americans but this does not mean that heart disease must follow. Your blood pressure should be kept down to approximately 120/80. If it consistently exceeds this level by a significant amount it can be life-threatening. If you find that you have consistently high blood pressure, take off any excess weight. Even in children, excess weight can cause an abnormal rise in blood pressure.

The other response is to reduce your salt intake. Americans notoriously oversalt their food, by as much as three times or more than what is naturally found in food which is adequate for your dietary needs. Hypertension is not necessarily caused by excess salt in your diet. But for maybe one out of every two Americans salt could be an important factor. It is recommended that you halve your regular salt intake. Don't place a salt shaker on the table and use less of it when preparing your meals. Note that commercial hamburgers are particularly high in sodium, as are of course many other fast foods. In addition, items like tomato juice, canned soups and vegetables are heavily presalted.

Another possible preventive response to hypertension is exercise, particularly aerobic exercise. There will be a lengthy discussion of exercise in Chapter 5, but it should be emphasized here that exercises that promote increased and sustained levels of oxygen consumption can eventually lower the set-point of your "normal" blood pressure. Not all exercise is prudent if you have high blood pressure; therefore any exercise program should be monitored by your cardiologist.

People with high blood pressure are five times more likely to have a heart attack than are people whose blood pressure is normal. If you learn that your blood pressure is up, then, with the assistance of your physician, examine all of the possible physical risk factors or causes of the hypertension that may exist in your daily life. Signs of concern should include excess caffeine use, excessive snoring (apnea), a diet that is high in animal fats and cholesterol, and, of course, cigarette smoking.

The principal means of lowering blood pressure is through drugs, and this is particularly true of very high blood pressure. Medication does not eliminate the cause of high blood pressure but by controlling it with drugs we reduce the risks associated with hypertension. This is effective only while the medication is being taken. It is advised that the medication be taken regularly and exactly as prescribed. Unfortunately many people don't. One reason is that some medications produce unpleasant side effects. However, there are more than two dozen medications that might be used and chances are your physician can find one that controls your blood pressure without causing the unwanted side effects.

The following is a list of many reasons people fail to comply with the prescribed procedure regarding their medication.

- They do not understand why the drug has been prescribed or how it is to help them;
- They are concerned over becoming dependent on the drug;
- They take medication only when they feel sick;
- It tastes unpleasant;
- Multiple medications mean multiple schedules which results in confusion;

If any of these applies to you, be advised that noncompliance or incorrect use can cause the medication to be ineffective and your problem to worsen.

The "Type-A" Personality

Handling stress effectively means also that you avoid those psychological risk factors that can create serious health problems. Your behaviors, particularly under stress, may seem fixed and involuntary; you may think that you can't help responding in any other manner. This is not necessarily true. Yes, you do have a *preferred response,* but it was once learned and it is possible to partially, if not completely, displace that response. If one key theme can be said to characterize the advice in this book it is that the role of self-awareness in the management of stress is paramount. This is true of any area of personal management. If you are to avoid the discomfort of stress or the more crippling and life-threatening illnesses related to unmanaged stress you must become more involved in the process of protecting yourself. Self-awareness is the key.

So far we have talked about physical risk factors that perhaps are more easily identified and controlled. But psychological risk factors and in particular specific behavior patterns have only recently gained attention as possible causes of stress and stress-related illnesses. One such behavior pattern is what cardiologists call *Type A Personality* or behavior.

Type A behavior could be described as hurried, impatient, controlling, aggressive, and easily angered.

By no means does this list exhaust all of the anxious and tense features of a Type A, but after considering these you should be able to add some of your own.

● Doing two or more things at one time. While listening to someone you are actively thinking of something else. A good example is the man who shaves and eats simultaneously, while reading an office report or memo. This is called polyphasic thought.

● Walking, talking, eating rapidly.

● Feeling impatience with the slowed pace of other people's conversation, you hasten it along by urging them to get to the point or finish their sentences or thought. You admire the patience of the driver behind you but not the driver in front of you. The idea of standing in a line drives you to serious distraction.

● You always bring the conversation around to those subjects which are especially interesting to you. Listening means hearing others respond to your subjects.

● You find you must often physically emphasize through gestures such as banging the table or pounding your fist into the palm of your other hand.

● You have little free time because it is impossible to arrange it, and when you do have it...it just looks unplanned and wasted.

● You have felt often that if you can't own it you don't want to know it.

● The only way you can understand and thereby appreciate something is to know the bottom line.

You might be tempted to ask what is so terrible about Type A behavior. Once again, it is believed by a growing number of cardiologists to be a major cause of heart disease.

As Doctors Friedman and Rosenman point out in *Type A Behavior and Your Heart,* "no bacterium, no virus, and no tumor has or ever will be found to be responsible for the coronary artery disease that at least 100 million Americans now harbor in some degree." Their point is that heart disease results from a constellation of conditions, both physical and psychological, one of which is the Type A behavior pattern. As the authors point out, most Type A subjects sooner or later develop or exhibit many of the following factors:

- A higher serum cholesterol;
- a higher serum fat;
- more diabeticlike traits;
- excessive cigarette smoking;
- little exercise (no time to do it);
- excessive strain on their endocrine glands (including adrenal glands), which can damage coronary arteries;
- a diet rich in cholesterol and animal fat;
- high blood pressure.

Adding to the alarm list is that the behaviors of Type A people are usually chronic, a more or less continuous struggle. Therefore they discharge greater amounts of norepinephrine (a nerve hormone discussed in Chapter 6) which is stress related. They also take as much as four times as long as normal to rid their blood of dietary cholesterol after each meal.

The list of potential risks the serious Type A subjects himself/herself to is far greater than mentioned here. But the last one we will mention is that through overstimulation of their sympathetic nervous system excess insulin can begin to accumulate in the blood.

What to do if you suffer from this "hurry sickness"? There is no easy answer because so much of Type A behavior is grounded in a world view. It expresses so much of that the individual feels about himself and others. However, this doesn't rule out the fact that many of these people don't realize how thoroughly hurried they are and what a poor management style they have adopted to accomplish their very important goals.

Perhaps the first thing to do is, once again, identify what your goals are, what you want them to be (and perhaps what they should be), and then assess the gap that exists between these two considerations. This can be done alone, but with the help of others you'll be pleasantly surprised at the greater richness and objectivity you can achieve. Think particularly about what is worth *being,* not what is worth *having.*

Think of the *quality* time you can spend with others in your life and how that time might serve them as well as you. Learn to listen to them, not just to confirm what you know about them, but for what you do not as yet know.

Think of the quality time you spend with just yourself. Your interior life left unattended can exaggerate the pressure of your exterior life. This is the balloon law: Equal pressure means less distortion and a steadier rise.

The following thought may at first seem a far remove from stress management for the Type A personality, but its wisdom should be considered by everyone, particularly those in a hurry.

> Nothing worth doing is completed in our lifetime; therefore, we must be saved by hope. Nothing true or beautiful or good makes complete sense in any immediate context of history; therefore, we must be saved by faith. Nothing we do, however virtuous, can be accomplished alone; therefore, we are saved by love. No virtuous act is quite as virtuous from the standpoint of our friend or foe as from our standpoint. Therefore, we must be saved by the final form of love which is forgiveness.
>
> —Reinhold Niebuhr

A more specific tactic to cure your "hurry sickness" is to revise your daily and weekly schedules, but only after you have decided upon goals that are worth salvaging because they directly affect your true well-being.

Think about the difference between analog time (the clock with hands and a face) and digital time (faceless). One says "it is approximately before or after," whereas the other only says "now now now." It is the difference of being "timely" and "prompt." Speed kills reflection. If you eventually learn to become sensitive to your own rhythms and needs, you will have less reason to allow your life to be determined by schedules, other people, and machines. Clocks were made for your and not vice versa. Even in a competitive business timeliness is superior to empty efficiency.

Any strategy that allows you more time to conduct your complete life will help. Therefore, if many of your activities seem too important to be eliminated from your schedule, then start them earlier and leave more time to accomplish and *enjoy* them. This also allows for delays that won't seriously disrupt. And if your plans must be or are changed, always have an alternative plan available.

The alternative activity includes having something to read, for example, or a problem or pleasant task to mentally organize, when standing in line or in traffic.

When making up your schedule always rank your tasks in order of importance with the understanding that it is possible that many tasks can't be completed, certainly those added tasks of others. However, every effort should be made to design a schedule that includes only those tasks that can be completed by you at the end of the day (learn to allot the appropriate amount of time to complete a task) and not those that must be but can't be. When your list continually shows items uncompleted it probably reflects your misuse of your own schedule. It should reflect what can and will be done, comfortably and in a timely way.

For example, if you work in an office, the telephone should also be managed. You may choose to place your own calls, but if you have an assistant he or she should take the incoming calls, and rate the order of their importance. You know more about the value of your time than does the caller. Regard your telephone as you do your mail: Some calls (or letters) are more important and immediate than the rest, some less.

Dealing with the Other Factors

We've now looked closely at certain of the risk factors, and cited some specific ways to deal with them. As for the many other behaviors or negative attitudes that represent "psychological" risk factors, if you take an honest inventory they will usually be uncovered, if they are not already known. But what to do about them?

Once again, it may not be easy and you may dispute the value of making any changes, even if they were possible. However, it is a valid stress-management strategy *to consider*, at least, changing specific attitudes, even if they seem principally insignificant or cosmetic. Besides, no one "in their right mind" wants to, or can, defend the unhealthful values of hopelessness, repressed feelings, isolation, or meaningless activities and relationships. The tips that follow may be of some help in considering changes toward some of those stress-related attitudes that in extremity can be a serious psychological risk factor.

How difficult some of your circumstances seem may be partially a case of your language. What you may term a "disaster" or "failure" can exist at the same time as knowledge or new data, a lesson well learned. It does take the brave soul to look at true disaster and rummage among its ruins for salvage, but that is what is required no matter the gravity of the circumstances. Though only an adage, it is nonetheless true that "it is the ill wind that does not blow some good." Few winds are truly ill: Gratitude and a willingness to start again eventually produce dividends from virtually all circumstances.

Learning to accept that which you cannot control is a life-long task, but its mastery is absolutely necessary to your survival. It can be painfully frustrating (though sometimes amusing) to see a young child struggle in its inability to distinguish between that which it can reasonably expect to master at a given time in its development and that which it cannot. For an adult it is never amusing and, if sufficiently serious, such frustration can lead to serious consequences. If you learn to live your life within the boundaries of your own gifts its struggles will never be futile. That is not to say don't take chances. Rather, take on new challenges with patience and at a pace appropriate to you.

Self-affirmation and self-belief come through constant efforts; eventually results will follow. First faith in yourself, and then belief. Remember, any attitude that undermines self-worth isn't interested in listening to change or new opportunities. Its only belief is that it knows all it will ever need or can know about itself. "No one can make you feel inferior without your consent." One question you may ask of yourself is what messages are you telling yourself each day? Are they positive? Do you know any positive thoughts or maxims that could apply or appeal to you? Find some; the useful wisdom of the world can be found in many of them.

Often the scale in which we see our problems is so small that it intensifies them, like a tempest in a teapot. To get relief from the captive pressure of some of your problems you must leave them temporarily behind so that you can truly see them. Two methods come to mind. Imagine advising someone else with the same problem bearing down upon them. In this situation you need not accept your limitations when advising this imaginary friend. It permits you to stretch for solutions while you listen to your own counsel.

The other healer is humor, laughter. The prominent magazine publisher and author Norman Cousins has written persuasively of his own experience using laughter to change the "inevitability" of some of his conclusions about a grave health problem, many of which he was told to accept by medical professionals. It is probable that you already take some of your own problems "too seriously."

Most problems are filled with incongruities and inconsistencies, the grist of humor. Laughter allows you to get outside of the problem or yourself so you can see both and consider anew what you and your unexplored resources can do regarding another solution. A sure test of how little imagination people bring to their problems, and how helpful it can be (or could have been), is to imagine a problem you had, years ago, that would have been helped by some imaginative and lighter solution. Your most embarrassing moments? How would you have handled your first date or first job interview with hindsight and a little imagination?

Coronary Heart Disease Risk Profile

The medical community does not yet have, and may never have, all the data from epidemiologic studies (and others) to show an absolute cause-and-effect relationship between the risk factors in this chapter and heart disease (or other stress-related disabilities). We have, however, provided evidence we believe sufficient to convince you that it would be dangerously foolish not to act prudently and reduce some of these risks.

The following Coronary Heart Disease Risk Profile from the National Foundation for Prevention of Disease does measure some degree of likelihood of a coronary event occurring in your life. You should have all the data required to complete this profile readily available, especially if you are over the age of forty-five. If not, it can be gathered from your physician or in a routine physical examination.

Complete the profile, and regard the results not as a threat but a challenge. In the chapters that follow, we will see further specific ways in which you can deal with the bad news stress can threaten you with. The easiest way to determine your profile is to do the following:

First, at the lower left, select the first risk factor, cholesterol. Move up the appropriate column (male or female) until you reach your known level. Move left and you will see your level or value (low to very high) and a point score. If your cholesterol reading is 250, as a male, your level is considered high and your point score is 10 points. Record them at the bottom of that column. The same is to be done for all the other risk factor considerations from HDL (high-density lipoproteins) to your age on the far right. When finished, enter your total point score and weigh it against the provided scale at the bottom of the chart.

CORONARY HEART DISEASE RISK PROFILE

RISK OF HEART ATTACK

POINTS		SEX		TOTAL CHOLESTEROL		HDL CHOLESTEROL		TRI-GLYCERIDE		SMOKING NO. CIGS/DAY		BLOOD PRESSURE SYSTOLIC		BLOOD PRESSURE DIASTOLIC		GLUCOSE		BODY FAT%		URIC ACID		EXERCISE		STRESS		FAMILY HISTORY STROKE OR HEART ATTACK		AGE	
		F	M	F	M	F	M	F	M	F	M	F	M	F	M	F	M	F	M	F	M	F	M	F	M	F	M	F	M
15	VERY HIGH			-260	280	35	25	180	220	30	30	150	160	105	110	125	125	42	35	8.0	9.0	NONE	NONE	CONSTANT HIGH STRESS		2 OR MORE BEFORE AGE 50		60	60
10	HIGH			-290	250	45	36	150	175	20	20	135	150	95	100	120	120	33	28	6.0	8.0	OCCASIONAL		FREQ. HIGH STRESS		1 BEFORE AGE 50		50	50
5	MODERATE			-220	230	56	45	125	150	10 PAST ONLY STOPPED 1 YR. AGO		125	140	85	90	110	110	29	23	5.0	7.0	3 TIMES PER WEEK		FREQ. MILD TO MOD. STRESS		1 OVER AGE 50		45	40
0	LOW			-200	200	80	70	100	110	10 YRS AGO		115	120	80	80	105	105	23	18	4.5	6.0	5 TIMES PER WEEK		OCC. MILD STRESS		NONE		40	30

RISK FACTORS	YOUR VALUE	POINTS

National Foundation for Prevention of Disease
Houston, Texas
© 1981

TOTAL POINTS

RISK: VH H M L (CIRCLE ONE)

LOW	0-29
MODERATE	30-59
HIGH	60-89
VERY HIGH	90+

Chapter

4 Defenses Against Stress:

Mind/Body Responses to Stress Exposure

We discussed in the preceding chapter the fact that many personal risk factors can add to the gravity of the health consequences of almost any stress exposure. Just as a heightened awareness of those consequences should lead you to make changes to lessen your overall risk, a greater sensitivity to your own stress symptoms is equally important before any intelligent discussion of appropriate techniques or programs for stress reduction. Many people, for many reasons, deny, or are unable to recognize in themselves, those behaviors or symptoms that are stress producing and are the cause of discomfort in their lives.

Not all of us share the same level of self-awareness when it comes to recognizing signs of trouble in ourselves. We see what we look for, which means if it troubles us to discover signs of failing health due to stress effects we probably won't.

Women seem to be more open to identifying and accepting possible stress symptoms, whereas many men, placing a premium on the appearance of control, are slow to acknowledge threatening signs. To acknowledge stress is to lose something.

The largest number of people seeking treatment for stress-related problems at the Harvard University Medical Clinic are women; but those treated there who are in far greater difficulty are men. Often their problems have progressed much further than the women's by the time they decide to secure treatment.

There is no checklist thorough enough to cover everyone's possible stress symptoms. But the inventories you used in Chapter 2 should be helpful when alerting to areas or sources of stress. As for signs of symptoms, most people, when prepared to honestly look, are able to make their own list, sometimes with the assistance of ours. When most people speak of stress symptoms they refer to rapid heartbeat, elevated blood pressure, short temper, crying jags, insomnia, impotence, asthma attacks, drinking, upset stomach, and instances of anxiety and depression.

Therefore, it is recommended at this juncture to make your own list of stress symptoms, generally negative responses that have grown out of specific stress.

Now that you have drawn some attention to the area(s) which reflect tension symptoms in your life it might be appropriate to look at those that disturb you the most and then see some of the techniques that are available to you for relief. We will be unable to discuss all of them in great detail in this book, but it is important for you to know the extent of the options available to you. One of those options is your personal physician, because many of the symptoms you may uncover could have strictly physiological origins requiring medical attention as a part of their management.

Just as everyone reacts to stress differently, so does

everyone react differently to relief techniques. Consequently the following suggestions are just that: *suggestions*. You may learn through trial and error that some other technique is more suited to your symptom than what is indicated. Furthermore, it is in combination that the mind and body exercises in this book are most effective. You will also note that though there are several techniques for any one category of symptom, the

TECHNIQUE EFFECTIVENESS CHART

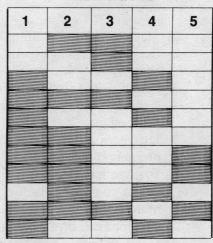

SYMPTOMS — **TECHNIQUES**

Symptom	1	2	3	4	5
Mental Fatigue		▓	▓		
General Fatigue		▓	▓		
Trouble Getting to Sleep	▓			▓	
General Anxiety	▓	▓		▓	
Specific Anxiety	▓			▓	
General Depression	▓	▓			
Tension Headaches	▓	▓			▓
Muscle Tension	▓	▓			▓
Obsessive Thoughts				▓	▓
High Blood Pressure	▓	▓			▓
Gastrointestinal	▓	▓			

Key

Jacobson Deep Muscle Relaxation Procedure	**1**
Meditation Exercises	**2**
Deep Breathing Exercises	**3**
Thought-Stopping Drill	**4**
Biofeedback Procedures	**5**

principal technique most frequently recommended is the Jacobson Deep Muscle Relaxation. Therefore it is the one technique we will spend the most time with in the latter part of the chapter.

Some combination of these five techniques which we will discuss individually in this chapter are generally effective when dealing with the following symptoms.

Whether the technique employed is a relaxation technique (to condition the body) or stress reduction technique (to condition the mind to handle stress), the intended therapeutic value (grouped under the heading of stress management) is to achieve some or all of the following skills in dealing with stress:

1. Mastery (your development of expertness)
2. Capacity to change (your ability to cope with planned change)
3. Patience (the first virtue of self-control)
4. Generalization (your small success may breed other success)
5. Distraction (your ability to get away from your problems)
6. Positive habits (necessary compensation for the bad habits you are replacing)
7. Maintaining interpersonal relations (tension and stress reactions can break down interpersonal relationships)
8. Self-Awareness (the function of feelings—"He is in touch with himself.")
9. Self-Expression (the lack of it generates frustration)
10. Symptom Relief (the most important short term objective)

Again, it has been observed that men, rather than women, set performance goals that are too high. They decide impatiently that if the task or relaxation technique is valid it *must meet their performance expectations*, even if they are unreasonable. Therefore, beware of goals that can't be met reasonably and soon. Deferred results are just as bad as no results. So don't ask for the improbable and don't wait interminably for it. A failed expectation can cause great damage to initial commitment; a perfectly acceptable result may be judged falsely as a failure simply because some other result was expected, or demanded. And what may happen is the program or sustained commitment may be abandoned in the belief that the technique doesn't work, when in truth it wasn't *used properly*. In short, be patient, but also be reasonable in establishing goals. They should be attainable sooner rather than later, and you can always set new goals once the first ones have been reached.

The Jacobson Relaxation Procedure

The first relaxation-response technique with which we will deal was developed by a man named Edmund Jacobson. The Jacobson Relaxation Procedure was also the first widely accepted deep-muscle relaxation technique used by professionals, and now laymen. It is designed to identify the different muscle groups where tension resides and eliminate that tension. The four muscle areas are: (1) hands, forearms, and biceps; (2) head, face, and neck; (3) chest, stomach, and lower back; (4) legs, calves, and feet.

There is no specified length of time you should practice this procedure, but it is recommended that you have several sessions daily for a week or more. Eventually you will use a more abbreviated procedure (shown later), once you have adjusted to and you have gained some benefit from the full Jacobson Procedure.

If possible the directions should be read to you or you should record them on tape so that they can be played back to you as you go through the procedure. This way you can concentrate upon just hearing and responding to the commands and you can keep your eyes closed as well. It is not absolutely required, but best results are achieved if you can lie down on a firm surface and loosen any constricting garments, including shoes. If you are reading the instructions yourself, the numbers in parentheses are suggested interval pauses (measured in seconds), but you should work at the pace that proves most comfortable for you.

Jacobson Relaxation Procedure

The discomfort of muscular tension makes us acutely and painfully aware of certain muscle groups. Through this procedure of applying systematic focused tension on selected muscles you will be able to identify and relax specific, often hard to get at trouble spots. However, this seemingly contradictory physiological technique of first tension and then relaxation allows you not only to single out specific tense muscles but also to achieve total body relaxation.

In preparation for the full procedure set aside at least twenty minutes. Get as comfortable as possible given the circumstances. It is preferable if you can remove your shoes, loosen any constricting garments, and lie on the floor.

Relax to the best of your ability. Imagine a rising column of mercury (not unlike that of a thermometer) that is graded with numbers that range from 0 to 100. Zero represents a completely tension-free state while 100 represents the most tension you have ever experienced. Now imagine which number you are right now and watch the column rise to that point. If you feel you must adjust it, to get a true reading, do so. During the procedure periodically you will be asked to take a reading, all in an effort to lower that column as close to zero as is possible.

Now, as you relax clench one of your fists, tighter and tighter for five seconds (5). Hold it clenched and feel the tension radiate in your fist, hand and forearm for five more seconds (5). Now release your grip. Feel the contrast in your loose fingers for four seconds (4). Now concentrate on relaxing your entire body for five seconds (5).

Once more clench the same fist tightly (4). Hold your grip and study the details of the tension as far up the arm as it goes (4). Release your grip and allow the tension to run out your fingers (4).

Now repeat the same procedure with your other fist while trying to relax all the other muscles. The only deliberately tensed muscles are those of your fist. And each time you release any tension concentrate on allowing it to flow away from that area out of your body.

After completing the exercise for the other fist, clench both simultaneously. Steadily apply tension to both fists and forearms up to your elbows (5). With your eyes shut imagine what they look like with the muscles bunched and more prominent (5). Release them slowly, straighten out your arms and feel the warming relaxation as if your fingers were resting in a bowl of warm water (10).

Bend your elbows and slowly tense your biceps and hold them (10). Lower your arms and allow them to relax (7). Always be conscious of the pleasant contrast between the tense and relaxed states of your muscles. Once more tense your biceps and feel them swell as you bunch them up (10). Relax, lower your arms and feel how more dense the muscles seem, while your arms may feel actually lighter, freer (10).

Now you will work higher up your arms to the triceps.

Straighten your arms and stretch them as far as they will go and then lock your elbows. You should feel the tension in the tricep muscles along the back of your upper arms. On the other side is the bicep (6). Release and return both arms to a comfortable position (10). Those two muscles may initially throb if you tensed them sharply, but they will grow heavy and warm in seconds. Repeat the procedure but hold the tricep taut for 10 seconds this time before releasing. Now relax your arms by imagine letting go of each muscle, from your fingers up to your triceps, but don't tense them. On the contrary, imagine not being able to feel anything in them at all (10).

Call up in your mind that tension column you began with and first take a reading and then try to lower it still further as you feel your body sink into a deeper state of relaxation and immobility.

Now you are going to work on your entire face and head. First wrinkle up your forehead and feel the scalp tighten (5). Now smooth it out and relax (3). Frown and crease your brows (5). Release (3). Open your mouth as wide as you comfortably can and then draw your upper lip down over your teeth (6). Release and feel the fullness in the skin around your mouth and nose (6). Close your eyes tightly and study the awareness you have through the tension (7). Relax (4). Now clench your jaws and bite down on your teeth (6). Release and let go of all those facial muscles you just tensed. Part your lips slightly and relax your tongue (10). Now press your tongue firmly against the roof of your mouth and feel the tension, even at the base of your tongue (7). Allow your tongue to return to a comfortable position (4). Purse your lips tightly (7). Then release them and feel the tingling sensation (5). Now imagine letting your facial muscles become so loose and relaxed that they could almost fall off through their own weight.

Take another reading of your diminished tension level and then imagine floating on water and bring that column down a few more points.

Now you are going to attend to those muscles that seemingly hold up your relaxed head. Press your head back as far as you can and hold it there (7). Roll it slowly to the left and hear the muscles stretch (5). Return to the center and roll your head to the right (5). Straighten your head and bring it forward, pressing your chin against your chest as much as possible (5). Now allow your head to return to a comfortable position and feel the warmth in those muscles (7). Shrug your shoulders and hold them in this position (7). Drop them and study the loosening sensation (7). Shrug them again and move them forward and back or in circles (7). Drop them and relax (7). Feel the relaxation radiate throughout your shoulders. Imagine your head being supported only by your spine and not your neck and shoulder muscles. As you allow yourself to be drawn into this state of relaxation, as if it were a body of water, think about how comfortable you feel all over . . . your neck, scalp, face, inside your mouth, and your arms. The sensation should be of added heaviness because you are not supporting those muscles any longer.

With your mouth relaxed, breathe through your nose and make yourself conscious of how free and easy your breathing has become. Particularly feel the sensation of being able to comfortably exhale any residual tension (10). Now you are going to breathe deeper. Relax your chest and place your hands on your stomach. Now as you drawn the air deep into your lungs feel your stomach rise but not your chest. Then as you continue to draw air your chest will rise as you finish filling your lungs (7). Hold your breath (7). Exhale slowly. Do not gasp (7).

Now place your arms alongside your body and repeat this breathing exercise (17). After you have expelled the air, breathe lightly and describe the feeling of relaxation (10). Repeat the exercise, but this time when you exhale imagine that tension column coming down as you release the air in your lungs (17).

Take about 20 seconds and review the relaxation steps throughout your body, muscle by muscle.

Tighten your abdominal muscles so that your abdomen is as hard as you can make it, but do not hold your breath or tense any other part of your body (10). Release the tension (5). Repeat the process (15). Notice how those muscles of your stomach seem more relaxed and settled.

Draw your stomach in as if you were trying to touch your spine (6). Release (5). Draw your stomach in again and hold it even longer but breathe as quietly as possible (10). Release (5). Now do the opposite. Push your stomach out. Do not hold your breath (7). Release (5). The sensation should be one of warmth. Notice how the relaxed stomach affects the chest and shoulders. As the tension dissolves the relaxation grows deeper and spreads throughout your body.

Arch your back making your lower back hollow. Do not pull your shoulders back. Continue to relax them by allowing them to drop. Concentrate only on your spine and lower back (10). Relax and settle into a comfortable position. Do not concern yourself with "good" posture (10). Repeat the procedure and feel only the muscular detail in your back (12). Relax completely (10). Flex your buttocks and thighs. If you are in a seated position press your heels down (6). Relax (6). Again, flex and relax (12). Do not hurry any of these exercises. They are intended to soothe you, leisurely. Bunch your toes to flex your calf muscles, or if you are sitting bring your feet on to your toes (8). Release them (6). Turn your toes upwards so as to flex your shins (8). Release them (6). If your shoes are removed firmly massage each foot for 5 seconds.

Now in reverse order, close your eyes and concentrate on further relaxing each muscle area starting with your feet and ending with your hands. Take your time.

Now check your reading on that tension column and see how close it is to zero. Remember, if your body lets go the column will fall to the bottom.

The full Jacobson Procedure may require as much as twenty minutes to complete. It is not recommended that you hurry the procedure simply to save time. You must devote the time necessary to do it at a proper, effective pace. With some initial success with the full procedure, shorter techniques will produce many of the same results without demanding as much time out of your day. But your body must be taught to relax, its muscles to let go. With patience and practice your muscles, after a successful exercise, will feel heavy, warm, and inert. It will be a pleasant sensation and your forehead should feel cool to the touch. Each time you perform the technique you'll achieve relaxing results in a shorter period of time. In fact, once you become familiar with the technique's ability to produce those results, the following drill allows you to relax almost upon demand.

1. Lie on your back in a quiet room. If convenient, remove your shoes and loosen any constricting garments. Relax.
2. Tense, or stretch, all the muscles of your body, working down from your face, neck, shoulders, arms, hands, stomach, thighs, calves, and your feet. Hold them fixed, if possible, for 6 to 10 seconds. Then release them and allow the "pieces" of your body to sink into the floor.
3. Draw in as much air as is comfortable, hold it for a second or two and then release it without gasping.
4. Repeat steps 2 and 3.
5. If you notice any tense muscle groups at this point, tense them separately as in step 2 and then release them.

As was suggested for the initial use of the Jacobson Procedure you might well benefit from the use of relaxation tapes. A variety of them are available, some of which provide additional technique instructions while others offer soothing remarks and music. One of the attractions of a tape is the opportunity it provides for you to just surrender to its message, to let go, to let your body and mind retreat to some place of comfort it seeks.

The Mental Relaxation Drill

Once you have achieved some success with muscle relaxation you are ready for another procedure, the Mental Relaxation or Meditation Drill. The muscle relaxation and the meditation drill are interactive, they support each other, and so it is recommended that you begin with the muscle relaxation exercise before using the Meditation Drill. As your body is to be clear of tension, so must your mind.

This drill can be useful whenever you are uncomfortably tense. You can do it whenever you have the need to do so. But it is recommended that you practice the relaxation drills before your meals (there is some natural hunger tension that you may find can be tempered making it possible to eat your meal more slowly and with greater comfort) and not any sooner than one hour after your meal.

Meditation Exercise

After you feel sufficiently relaxed from the muscle relaxation exercise, remain in the same position, close your eyes, and allow your forehead to become cool.

1. Remove all thoughts from your mind and allow it to wander aimlessly. As if your mind was a muscle, permit it to relax and "settle to the bottom."
2. As thoughts occur, reject them. You can do it verbally, or you can imagine an image of cleansing.
3. Picture a clean surface without detail, a wall or sky. If you dream in color, try cool blue.
4. Now take note of the weightlessness of your body and

its slow rhythmic breathing as cool air passes through it.

5. If you don't feel calm and relaxed try an incantation, a slow repetition of a word whose sound you find soothing. If the room is absolutely silent try listening only to the sound of your breathing. Eventually you want an image of leaving your body and mind behind.

There may be many occasions in which you may not be able to defend yourself against an intrusive and obsessive thought, particularly one that preys on your mind and causes anxiety. In those instances to further support both your meditation skills and growing sense of self-control, consider this exercise.

1. Reach a satisfactory muscle and mental relaxation level.
2. When the persistent thought returns instruct it to leave; say no to it. Continue to do so each and every time it returns while taking comfort in the security of your relaxation state. The obsessive thought will grow weary and less frequent.
3. As your confidence and success grow change the "no" to a silent rejection; mentally "turn it over" as if it were a picture. You'll find your mind growing less obsessive and less active during the relaxation process.
4. Fill your quiet mind with the picture of a calm and pleasant place—something out-of-doors such as the sky, the ocean, or an open empty meadow. Lie down in it.
5. When you feel free of any distracting thoughts change the view to a clean, featureless surface, or darkness if you want. But empty out your mind.
6. Now, let some color return, preferably the coolness of blue and think about how *relaxed* you are.

Deep Breathing Exercises*

The concept of breathing has a much broader meaning than is generally understood by most Americans. The activity of deep breathing, as opposed to shallow breathing, is not only to fill your lungs with fresh air and expel carbon dioxide and other wastes but to promote the proper circulation of nourishing oxygen to all body tissue through the blood system. By flushing your bloodstream with oxygen the cells of your body are revitalized, reserves of energy can be slowly gathered and directed through the body to strengthen your lungs and cause your heart to burn oxygen efficiently. Proper deep breathing can also calm and sedate you when distressed.

You may have noticed athletes, such as football players, inhaling oxygen during the game or their performance. This is because the fresh and concentrated source of oxygen alerts the muscles of their exhausted bodies. It also increases their mental alertness, for the brain burns a considerble amount of energy through its use of oxygen and sugar. An experiment conducted at a Veterans Administration Hosital in Buffalo, New York placed thirteen elderly men in a pressurized chamber and exposed them periodically to 100% oxygen. After two treatments each for two weeks the patients showed an increased performance of 25% on standard memory tests.

Despite the central role breathing plays in our lives as organisms, few of us have been taught how to breathe. Most of us are unaware of the fact that we use probably only a third of our lung capacity. Our breathing is shallow and occurs about fifteen to seventeen times a minute, taking in about a pint of air each time. Yet your lungs can hold eight times as

---

*Although the control of breathing is of no proven or probable value in disease prevention or in altering one's physiologic response to a given stress, there are many who believe it is of value as a technique to achieve relaxation and therefore to reduce the body's overall response to stressful situations.

much air. Therefore shallow breathing provides only limited amounts of fresh oxygen and doesn't fully expel all the burnt gases, such as carbon dioxide.

Eventually you will adopt drills or exercises that are convenient to your use. They don't take much imagination and the following is such an example:

1. If seated or standing make some effort to get comfortable.
2. Breathe deeply, drawing the air slowly as you relax your stomach muscles. Then let it expand and fill your lungs completely. Swallow, as if locking the fresh oxygen in your lungs, and hold it for six seconds. Now exhale slowly allowing all your muscles to relax, arms, neck and back. Repeat as often as convenient.
3. If it is convenient close your eyes (if you are standing it is probably not advisable in that you might become dizzy) and picture something pleasant, something or someplace that you associate with relaxation.

When under stress your oxygen needs may increase, evidenced in part by an accelerated heart rate. But if your breathing is shallow you may labor only to provide an inadequate supply.

The following breathing exercises are designed not only to improve your health in general and strengthen your heart and lungs, but also to provide some specific symptom relief. For example, studies indicate that deep-breathing exercises can temporarily reduce anxiety in specific situations, as well as in some instances of general or unspecified anxiety. Furthermore it can reduce the distress of anger or resentment and provide a feeling of mastery and renewed self-control. As mentioned earlier it also will eliminate some fatigue while reducing muscle tension.

If you had singing lessons in school as a child, you were probably told to breathe from your diaphragm. This permits you to take in more air and sing longer without losing volume or having to stop for more air. Your diaphragm is the principal muscle used in breathing. It forms the floor of your chest and when you breathe deeply the upper, middle, and lower portions of your lungs get a full supply of oxygen.

Air is first drawn deeply into your expanding diaphragm (relax your shoulders, your chest, and your solar plexus) and then it fills up the middle and upper reaches of your lungs. When you exhale the process is reversed. The suitable image is that of a pitcher being filled and emptied with water—bottom to top and top to bottom. Breathing in this fashion will eventually help you overcome lifetime habits of shallow and lazy breathing by getting more air into your lungs. Good deep breathing exercises massage your liver and spleen and help general circulation of your blood to your heart so blood can return to the lungs for more oxygen.

The first formal breathing exercise is to demonstrate simple diaphragmatic breathing. This procedure can calm nerves and, when carried out just before retiring at night, can induce more restful sleep.

1. You may stand, or lie face-up on the floor. Try to empty your mind of any distracting thoughts, relax your muscles, particularly your shoulders and chest, and loosen any restricting garments including your belt. Your abdomen must be completely free to permit full circulation of blood in that area.
2. Inhale deeply through your nostrils. Your inhalation and exhalation should be done slowly and evenly, and as silently as possible. Don't gasp for air; reach for it gracefully, but don't lunge.
3. First fill your expanding abdomen and then your lungs. Again through your nostrils, exhale the air in your

80

lungs and then draw your abdomen back to your spine expelling all of the gases at the bottom of your lungs.

4. This procedure should be repeated steadily, using the same rhythm, the same number of seconds each time.

Another breathing technique that has provided relief from the discomfort of *tension headaches* is the following:

1. Your position should be comfortable. You need not necessarily be lying down.
2. Place your right thumb firmly alongside of your right nostril and inhale deeply but slowly for 8 seconds through your left nostril, breathing diaphragmatically.
3. Swallow to lock in the air and close your left nostril with your little finger and hold for the same count of 8.
4. Release the pressure of your right thumb and exhale, slowly, for the same count of 8 seconds. The tendency will be to release the air suddenly, but don't. If you feel an intense need for fresh air reduce the number of seconds for the exercise.

    The procedure should be done rhythmically with a growing sense of control and stamina. Once you achieve a smooth flowing inhalation and exhalation using 8 seconds (that is a total of 24 seconds), begin to add more time to the entire procedure.

For those with a history of coronary problems this last breathing exercise is not recommended without the advice of their personal physician. Its purpose is to introduce greater amounts of oxygen to your blood system than what is taken in during the course of normal breathing, or any of the earlier exercises. Because of the sharp increase of oxygen it often helps to relieve the effects of some early depression. This is also an exercise that will take some time to master and even then can always be improved upon.

1. Sit comfortably in a chair and close your eyes.
2. Exhale forcefully through your nose; at the same time, draw your abdomen in expelling air. Virtually blow the air out.
3. After the first thrust release the contraction of your abdomen and your lungs will take in fresh air through your mouth. You need not consciously inhale. This is a voluntary action. Just concentrate on expelling the air.
4. You want to achieve a steady staccato rhythm, not hurried. Try ten expulsions and then relax and breathe luxuriously, deeply.
5. First do groups of ten in sets of 4 or 10. Then you can build the length of the set to a hundred or more, or to as many as you think will benefit you.

Be aware that initially you may feel dizzy, but that will pass as your skill increases. Also your abdomen muscles may be tender at first. This is also good and this will also pass.

Biofeedback Techniques

The knowledge that biofeedback exists has reached a broad segment of the general public, but biofeedback is still not properly understood by most people.

To begin, let's define it. *Feedback* may be defined as a method of changing a system's activity through self-monitoring of its ongoing performance. The monitoring is conducted through a *closed feedback loop* which allows results to be adjusted so as to satisfy whatever criteria are set. For example, the thermostat in your home or apartment is a feedback system. It detects or is fed the temperature changes in the room. When the temperature falls below a preset limit it "turns" the heating unit on; and when the temperature reaches the desired level it will "turn" the unit off. The system operates automatically.

The regulation of your body functions is made possible through numerous feedback loops, some conscious, others not. You perspire when the temperature changes, and your pupils dilate in response to a change in available light. At the same time, your body responds to the presence of certain bacteria and your adrenal glands secrete adrenalin when there is a change or the threat of one in your environment.

Furthermore, learning a new voluntary skill employs the use of feedback information. For example, the process of learning to play the piano requires that you hear the sounds produced by the striking keys if you are to confirm whether you must adjust your efforts or continue. Though they have never heard speech, individuals deaf from birth can learn to speak by watching lip movement and feeling the vibration of vocal cords. By "feeding back" the necessary information, in a different manner because of their handicap, they learn to speak that which they have never heard.

Biological feedback, or biofeedback, is the process of monitoring a specific physiological function and feeding back its activity to the person being monitored. By becoming conscious of this hidden function or process through *seeing* the results, you can learn to self-regulate the activity. Most biofeedback procedures are conducted initially in controlled circumstances, often in a laboratory with equipment that can sensitively monitor the activity, such as a computer. But there are other ways you can "view" the feedback that does not require a trained professional in a laboratory setting.

Whatever the biofeedback technique it should involve one or more of the following objectives:

1. The relief of your particular distress through the

retraining of a function that caused or contributed to your problem or disorder.

2. To recognize and discriminate states of tension versus relaxation. As we mentioned earlier many people have not learned to recognize these various states and their subjective impressions of something like deep relaxation may not correspond to an objective assessment of this response. For example, there are circumstances in which some people will believe they are relaxed when it is quite apparent to others that, quite to the contrary, they are tense. This is so because they probably have never learned what really deep relaxation is all about.

3. The ability to shift between a relaxed and an aroused state when appropriate. Relaxation on demand is the goal.

4. The last is the improvement of our self-responsibility resulting from our new-found control of previously unmanageable activity. It also adds to the ten therapeutic values we mentioned at the outset of the chapter.

Stress could be described as a hyperarousal state of one or more of your bodily systems. And stress is maladaptive when it occurs too frequently or is sustained too long; it can adversely affect your performance or result in a stress-related disorder. Everyone has what is referred to as a *preferred response* to stress. That is, under stress you are likely to "choose" to be hyperactive in a particular physiological system, consistently. For example, some people under stress will have cardiovascular symptoms (heart palpitations or hypertension) while others will have muscle-related symptoms (head or neck pains). The character of the stress does not necessarily govern what symptoms you will evidence.Studies show that given the same type of stress, people have a pattern of consistent responses that are peculiar to them. People will fall into different types in terms of which physiological system will be especially responsive. Therefore, for some it will be the muscle system, for others it will be their cardiovascular system, and for yet others it will be their gastrointestinal system. You may already know what is your preferred response, but many don't.

Additional studies have shown that we become so ingrained in our "preferences" that even during sleep or resting conditions we produce specific responses that are related to our type. For example, when ulcer patients were asleep their gastric secretions were three to twenty times as great as those of normal subjects. Headache patients, even on days when not suffering from an attack, have been found to have abnormal brain wave patterns about twice those seen in normal patients. So, we have responses that we favor, voluntarily and involuntarily, and these personal and preferred responses are a product both of genes and learned behavior. What biofeedback techniques permit is an opportunity to examine those responses and in some instances modify them. Though some are technically speaking involuntary they are not beyond our control, as thought not too many years ago.

There are two other elements of stress behavior that should be mentioned. Just because you react with an elevated heart beat and someone else develops an upset stomach, does not mean that it necessarily will lead to a disorder. However, if circumstances occur where there is a frequent triggering of this particular response in you, then trouble can develop. You'll recall that we spoke of the cumulative nature of stress, that a history of it may govern your ability to cope in the future. Studies demonstrate that many people who are prone to stress that raises their blood pressure constantly, are found to have changed their *set point*. In other words there may be a physiological mechanism by which frequent provocation can reset the resting level of your "normal" blood pressure.

The other element of your body's response to stress that will have some bearing on our biofeedback thinking is the failure of *homeostatic control.* All this means is that even though you may react initially the same way to stress as you may have in the past, if you have had a history of frequently triggering your "preferred" response your recovery rate may be slowed. A reasonably healthy person, in the face of some particular stress, should decrease their tension level in fairly short order once they begin to come to grips with it. *But* the tension levels of people who have been almost chronically stressed decrease very slowly and in severe cases do not decrease, but continue to increase. These unfortunate people suffer from a defect in homeostasis, their ability to reject the change and return to "normal." Of course this condition leads directly to stress-related illnesses or other disorders.

Biofeedback can play a very helpful role as sort of a "physiological retraining." Either with the assistance of a physiologist or employing home techniques, some of which we have already mentioned, you can relearn ways to relate to stress, to avoid what may be a maladaptive response to frequently occurring situations.

One thing you must examine as you utilize any biofeedback technique is whether your "preferred" response is being positively reinforced, thus raising the probability of the same response occurring again and again. For example, if you plan your time poorly and have to rush to meet a deadline, or cram for a test in school, and then do well, the positive result may reinforce the destructive behavior next time. And if the fear of failure fuels you as you approach the deadline, still not prepared, it is a double reinforcement, for you escape failure (one reward) and succeed (another reward).

The key to stress-related problems or disorders is the elicitation and reinforcement of your "preferred" response to stress by the stuff of everyday life. Through frequent triggering, your physiological response can grow more harmful, increasing your inability to cope with stress the next time.

Biofeedback can help. Among other things it can reduce

the intensity of your maladaptive response, speed the return of your system affected to a normal level after the stress-caused stimulation, and perhaps interdict the whole process and prevent any harmful response whatsoever.

Two basic approaches have grown out of this relatively new understanding of how you might create change or alter some features of your physiological responses. One is direct, in that it focuses on a specific symptom or response and attempts to change it. One example would be a problem like muscle tension in your shoulders or neck; an appropriate solution, or "feedback" technique, might be deep-muscle relaxation. By fixing upon the tension in that particular muscle group and employing that portion of the Jacobson procedure which deals with the tension response (by removing the constriction in the muscle) you would be using a direct symptom approach. In a biofeedback laboratory where a variety of monitoring technologies or equipment is available, a physiologist or medical professional can also employ several direct biofeedback techniques. They can teach you to actually modify your blood pressure or the gastric secretion in your stomach.

The other approach is less direct, not fixed upon a specific symptom or area of your body. This approach attempts to achieve something called *whole-body low arousal response.* All this means is that becoming thoroughly relaxed is a defense against stress production, regardless of whether the symptoms are specific or general. If you are completely relaxed you can't be tense. They are incompatible.

There is a good deal to be learned about this field, both by the professional and the layman, and this handbook can do little more than to make reference to it and offer a few techniques.

For some of the specific problems of stress, such as migraine headache, essential hypertension and general anxiety, treatment can be both direct and indirect. Despite the home-remedy look to all of the practices, they are grounded in scientific principles. For more than twenty years they have been in widespread clinical use, on a far more ambitious and complex scale than described here.

In laboratory settings using a direct method of feedback, a problem such as high blood pressure can often be successfully dealt with. Participants are "fed" back knowledge of their blood pressures at regular intervals through the use of an occluding cuff, a device that measures blood pressure. These participants meditate and deep relax, and, as a result of training, are able not only to lower their temporary blood pressure levels but establish new baseline levels, as much as 18% lower.

If you choose to create a direct approach program for home use, you should first consult your personal physician. Merely using one of the many blood pressure reading devices, now readily available and easy to operate, may not be sufficient. With the personal knowledge your physician has of your medical profile, he or she can create a monitoring program that will have meaning for you. For example, depending upon the time of day and adjacent activity (e.g., a meal or argument), your reading will probably vary. Now, in and of itself, this is not necessarily significant. But if not properly understood it could be the cause of undue alarm and could directly and adversely affect the next reading. But if you are capable of establishing a baseline picture of your blood pressure for various and scheduled times of the day, with the assistance of your physician, you can determine whether the readings have been correctly taken, whether the baseline requires some adjustment, and future readings can be measured against this parameter, the standard or baseline.

There are other devices now available for home use that can be used in a direct approach method of biofeedback stress reduction. One such instrument is the GSR 2 (Galvanic Skin Response). By converting minute tension-related changes in your skin pore size into sound, a palm-size level biofeedback monitor allows you to listen to and potentially control stress level readings. It is not a complicated apparatus, nor expensive, about the cost of a small portable radio. To use the GSR 2, you rest two fingers on its sensing plate; then you'll hear a specific pitch or tone. By learning to relax through any one of the methods we have talked about it is possible for you to lower the pitch, which indicates that you are lowering the electrical discharge on your skin which in turn is an indication of your lowering the activity of your nervous system.

Another tool that was developed for use in home practice in thermal biofeedback training is a thermochromic liquid crystal finger temperature indicator. Despite its long name, it, too, is quite simple and very inexpensive (it costs less than five dollars). It is a small piece of heat sensitive film, three inches by one, that is wrapped around the tip of your finger. It measures the surface temperature of the skin of your finger and, though it is primarily used to deal with circulatory disorders, it can effectively monitor temperature changes due to hypertension or general tension.

To repeat, however: Responsible and effective use of any biofeedback home equipment should include a consultation with your physician.

The reasons why relaxation and meditation favorably affect your body systems is too complex to be discussed here and in some instances medical science is not satisfied with some of its own answers. For example, there is no consensus as to why muscular relaxation should be useful in the treatment of anxiety. Yet test results show that it does. It has been speculated that muscle relaxation affects not only your muscle system but affects your other bodily systems as well. Simply stated it probably produces a physiological condition incompatible with anxiety. When you are relaxed you can't be tense.

Chapter

5 Displacement of Stress:

Exercise Strategies That Work

The Value of Physical Fitness

The pursuit of physical fitness is desirable for several reasons. The most important may be that you will live longer. But beyond that you will in all probability live *better* if you live an active physical life, with a better chance of fighting off disease.

A healthy body has a lot to do with whether we have a healthy emotional life as well. Though the health of one does not necessarily guarantee the health of the other, they cannot be separated. Recent studies suggest that aerobic exercise can positively affect your emotional makeup. Depending upon the program of exercise and its duration, it can actually elevate your mood. Some psychotherapists have found exercise an effective complement to psychotherapy for the treatment of mild depression.

91

There are still more potential benefits. Aerobic exercise can suppress your appetite. Almost all the hormones produced as a result of exercise are appetite suppressants: dopamine, noradrenaline, and serotonin. These hormones are so effective and so rapid in their action that when they are injected in animals, the treated creatures will stop eating even if they are hungry.

Physiologists refer to the effects of physical exercise as being *global*; the positive effects on your mind and body may be so varied and far-reaching that it is impossible to quantify and measure all of the individual effects. However, exercise does promote a sense of well-being by enhancing ego strength, dissipating anger and hostility, and relieving boredom. So if your mood is up, so may be your will to accomplish those things that can support your good feeling.

Of all the traditional stress reduction techniques, exercise may be the simplest and most effective. Your exercise program can strengthen your body, improve circulation, provide a sense of additional energy, and will best utilize the nutrients in the food you eat. Exercise also serves to produce a natural, post-exercise fatigue, which makes relaxation easier and helps to induce restful sleep.

As commonplace as exercise promotion may be there are many misconceptions about exercise; and there are some kinds and levels which may in fact be counterproductive to lessening stress and improving your body's general condition.

What Do You Know About Exercise?

1. The average person requires at least forty minutes of running a day (or some equivalent exercise) to stay healthy and conditioned.   TRUE or FALSE

2. Your exercise program provides no significant benefit towards maintaining or building muscular fitness unless and until you experience strain or fatigue.   TRUE or FALSE

3. If you experience pain during exercise, especially in the feet or legs, it is best to keep going and work through it. TRUE or FALSE

4. Running a mile uses less calories than walking a mile.   TRUE or FALSE

5. If you run or engage in other vigorous exercise, you need extra protein for energy and to build muscle.   TRUE or FALSE

6. If you perspire freely on a hot day, especially during exercise, you should take a salt tablet.   TRUE or FALSE

7. If you drink more than a swallow of fluid before you run or jog, or if you interrupt exercise to satisfy your thirst, you risk painful cramps.   TRUE or FALSE

8. If you exercise to lose weight, it is a good idea—in most weather—to wear loose-fitting clothing which covers the body and limbs, because it will help you avoid muscle cramps. TRUE or FALSE

9. A regular program of exercise conditioning is helped by the diet supplementation of vitamins and minerals. TRUE or FALSE

10. Eliminating as much sugar and starch from your diet as possible is one of the best ways to become fit through good nutrition, especially in conjunction with an exercise program. TRUE or FALSE

The correct answer to all of these questions is FALSE. We will address each of the issues raised by these questions in this chapter. But let us talk first about exercise in general.

What Is the Best Form of Exercise?

The correct answer to this question is that the best form of exercise for you is an activity to which *you* will stay committed. Invariably people lose their initial enthusiasm for specific exercise if they don't learn to enjoy it; if they can't comfortably incorporate it into their daily regimen they find reasons to drop it. What follows it is a loss of commitment to the purpose of the exercise program in the first place. Therefore, select an exercise that is appealing both because of the pleasure of the activity and its accessibility. For example, if your swimming pool were a twenty minute drive away, you most likely would soon have to confront the fact of its inconvenience. The best advice is to develop a series of exercises that you can juggle depending upon your schedule, mood and objective.

Aside from the problem of diminished commitment, the exercise that provides the really superior benefits, particularly for your stress prone heart, is an *aerobic* exercise. One important warning, however: If you are over thirty-five years of age and have not been exercising regularly, *have a medical checkup and discuss the exercise program with your physician.*

Does running a mile actually use less calories than walking a mile? On its face the answer to this question seems obviously to be false. But why? The answer is not that just the opposite is true; in fact, running a mile uses approximately the *same* amount of calories, not more and, of course, not less. Why this is true is that within a moderate range of activity the difference, as far as calories expended, is determined by the time spent exercising. If you walked a mile it might take you as much as four times as long to complete the mile than if you ran it. Understandably, if you were to run ten miles you would probably burn up more calories than walking the same distance because this is not moderate exercising and your "charged up" body would burn up additional calories for some time after you stopped running.

My point is that an exercise activity that raises your heart beat to a specific level, and burns oxygen at this rate for a minimum of twenty minutes, is of considerable value. This exercise is called aerobic. It increases the blood vessels' ability to carry oxygen, the muscles' ability to utilize oxygen, and improves the efficiency of your heart muscle and its ability to withstand not only the strain of future exercise but also its ability to handle other demands on it, such as stress.

The two most popular aerobic exercises are jogging and swimming. The latter is more enthusiastically recommended because it avoids the trauma to the legs and spine of jogging and utilizes the arms and chest muscles as well as the legs. It is done with the help, or buoyancy, of water. The gravitational force on your joints is not nearly so great as when standing out of water. Your weight in the water (with only your head and neck exposed) is only one-tenth what it is out of water.

Since the water, and not your body, bears much of your weight, swimming is an excellent exercise for those suffering with arthritis. At the same time the buoyancy also spares your knees, ankles, and lower back from the constant pounding associated with jogging. In fact swimming is often prescribed for those people who have suffered joint injuries from other sports or exercise activities. It strengthens the muscles of your abdomen and has been prescribed as the one exercise program for those with chronic back problems.

If you are out of shape or have not exercised in years, swimming is highly recommended. Besides the support from water's buoyancy, while swimming you are moving horizontally and your heart doesn't have to pump against gravity. This is a considerable benefit for the seriously overweight for whom exercise presents additional risks, especially during exercise. The more overweight you are, the more buoyant you are in water. In addition the excess amount of heat you generate because of this bulk is "dampened" by the cool water.

Aerobic exercise, particularly swimming, provides a constant and steady demand for oxygen on your heart, but that steady and continuous demand should not raise your heart beat beyond the *submaximal* target zone, or approximately 75% of the maximum rate. This submaximal rate can be easily estimated by subtracting your age from 220, and multiplying that figure by 75%. For example, if you are thirty-five your computation should look like this: $220 - 35 = 185 \times .75 = 139$ heart rate. Therefore, while exercising, your heart should not exceed this rate. This target range (with a 10% variance) establishes a general limit to protect you from placing an unnecessary and perhaps dangerous demand on your heart while indicating a target area within which you will most benefit from the conditioning your heart requires from aerobic work. One word of warning: If you take drugs that effect your heart rate, or have diabetes, this formula will be an overestimate of your maximum heart rate. In addition, if this target zone seems too strenuous, have a stress test to determine your "real" maximal heart rate.

"Isotonic" means constant pressure on your muscles from the flow and weight of the water. Through constant stroking swimming enhances muscle tone over most of your body and in particular can help counter varicose veins which pose circulation problems for many people in their later years. Another obvious benefit from constant swimming at a submaximal rate is calorie loss. Even though the sensation of cooling water disguises it, swimming is more demanding than most exercise activities in this regard.

Establishing a Swimming Regimen

Consumption of calories during swimming differs with the individual (owing to weight, speed, stroke used and skill level). Even the temperature of the water will have some bearing on calorie consumption. But a one-hundred-fifty-pound person who swims the crawl at twenty-five to fifty yards per minute could burn off as much as 750 calories in an hour. A similar consumption of calories occurs with the back or breast stroke, but the butterfly (at fifty yards per minute) will burn off 850 or more calories because it is so demanding.

As with any exercise program, the benefit you derive from swimming will be proportionately tied to the effort you put into it. You may be one of those many people who are not good swimmers or assume that any kind of recreational swimming will be adequate for conditioning purposes. Most people do not swim fast enough and far enough to get as much from it as they can from running. However, lessons are available at most Y's as well as at many health clubs.

If you find swimming pleasant you should develop a program that has as its goal a distance of a mile in less than forty-five minutes, or twelve hundred yards in thirty minutes. If you are a recreational swimmer, you should start with interval training. Try to swim fifty yards, take a three-minute break, swim fifty more yards, take another three-minute break, then swim a final fifty yards. Gradually, increase your distance and decrease your breaks, both in length and number. The greater the number of uninterrupted laps the better the conditioning but also the greater the likelihood of boredom, so don't risk losing interest in the activity for the sake of more distance. Also, during the break check your pulse by placing your hand lightly on the side of your neck, directly below your ear or on the inside of your wrist, right below the thumb. It is interesting to see during the three-minute break how much your heart rate drops in an effort to return to its resting rate. As your endurance improves you will notice the extent to which your body learns to adapt itself to and recover from its hard work.

Correcting Some Misconceptions

Before we go on to the subject of jogging I want to return briefly to those ten commonplace questions about exercise. As was noted the correct answer to all of the questions is FALSE. Regardless of the exercise you choose you should remember:

● The average person only requires approximately twenty minutes of running, or some other aerobic exercise, to enjoy its conditioning benefits and they need not experience strain and excessive fatigue.

● If you experience pain during your exercise, especially in the feet or legs, STOP. Pain is an early warning system that something is wrong and needs attention and relief.

● The next time you exercise you should stretch those sore muscles. Warm muscles are less subject to injury. Therefore, your excercise program begins, officially, with a warm-up. If you jog, start with a brisk walk or slow jog for a few minutes. And if it is swimming do some stretching out of the water. And when you finish your workout conclude the entire program with a cool-down period. If it is jogging repeat the warm-up procedure, a slow jog. Once your muscles cease their effort in the accelerated circulation, the demand falls primarily on your heart. So don't stop too abruptly.

● Vigorous exercise does not require extra protein in your diet, but perhaps extra carbohydrates for quick, fast-burning energy. The protein present in your diet therefore need not be consumed immediately and can be devoted to tissue building.

● It is not usually recommended to take a salt tablet in anticipation of perspiring freely. Your exercise is intended to cause perspiration and additional salt is not usually needed. In the case of extreme heat fatigue or asthenia (weakness), rest, drink plenty of fluids, and, if not counter-indicated by your physician, consume extra salt, but not as salt tablets.

● Drinking fluids before you run or jog insures that you will not unnecessarily dehydrate yourself and it will help keep your body temperature at the optimal level. Painful cramps might only result from excessive drinking of fluids before swimming or the drinking of exceptionally cold fluids immediately following a heavy running effort. Heavy, loose-fitting clothing does not affect whether or not you will get muscle cramps. Loose clothing helps you to start sweating during your warm-up and after that it helps you to sweat freely. However, in excessively warm weather you may wish to wear nylon because it does not retain the moisture and it will permit your overheated system and skin to cool itself. Running without any shirt in the wind can cause some muscles to cramp because the wind cools them down sharply while the blood carries more heat to the skin to be released. Also if you don't cover yourself immediately after running a chill is always possible. On a hot sunny day you should cover your head if you are bald, but knee-high socks are not recommended because it won't permit your ankles and calves to sweat freely. In this instance low cut socks or no socks are preferable.

● Adding vitamin and mineral supplements to your diet does not help your conditioning during any exercise program. All it does is give you a very expensive urine. And instead of eliminating sugar and starch from your diet it may be recommended to increase them if you are not overweight to supply you with an additional ready energy source if you feel depleted after your exercise.

Jogging for Health

Another valuable and accessible aerobic exercise is jogging or running. *Aerobics* comes from the Greek *aero* meaning "air," and, as with swimming and other such exercises, aerobic jogging has come to mean running to build up the intake of air, and the consequent strengthening of your oxygen dependent lungs, heart and cardiovascular system.

There is much and little to choose between swimming and jogging as a frequent aerobic exercise. They have their separate appeals and drawbacks. Some people find that the slow, pounding gait of jogging jars their feet, ankles, knees, and lower back, causing discomfort. Many joggers suffer knee or ankle problems from *pronation,* the rolling inward of the foot as it moves forward during the running gait which can cause injury to your ankles, knees, and hips. It is important that you wear the correct shoe for your needs.

If your feet bother you after jogging it is advised that you see your podiatrist or orthopedist, or at least a running shop that carries a wide range of specially built running shoes. Do not simply tolerate inadequate running shoes. While running, each shoe hits the surface about eight hundred times a mile and with a force three times your body weight. In total your feet are absorbing tons of impact and any abnormality in your foot structure or inadequacy of protection in the shoe you're wearing will be considerably heightened.

It is also a good idea to select your running surfaces carefully. Rather than running on cement or asphalt, try to find a softer surface such as grass, dirt, or cinders.

Jogging is aerobic, submaximal, and repetitious, three of the four conditioning features offered by swimming. And for many people it is about the most convenient and best general exercise to stay in shape and remain active. It doesn't require a special place (like a swimming pool) nor does it require any equipment beyond a pair of appropriate running shoes. And not unlike swimming it is not just something for your heart. It promotes overall fitness, elevates your mood and generally is an excellent physical (and perhaps psychological) defense against general stress.

It is difficult to list all of the benefits from regular aerobic exercise, and in particular, jogging or running. In many instances the benefits are peculiar to the individual participant. For example, a smoker or heavy drinker who quits is doing more for themselves than they would do by running. Yet for some people a commitment to run causes them to cut down and, in many cases, eliminate their smoking and drinking habits. People often will say that they started their exercise program because of a distressing physical examination or a friend or relative who had a heart attack, but they continue to run or swim because of a general attitude change. They experience an improvement in their own capacity and capability, a positive pro-active management posture toward the rest of life. This is not to say that one's life is subject to a conversion, but many people experience a new look at their capacity for modest change in their lives after some prolonged commitment to something like running. As some have put it, even if they were told that it wasn't providing any significant conditioning value for their body they would continue only because "they know how bad they will feel when they stop exercising."

Preparation is necessary for all strenuous exercises, but this is probably more true of jogging than most others. This is so because of the immediate and intense strain on various leg muscles and joints. Throwing these cold muscles into vigorous activity can result in strains and pulls, and once a muscle is weakened, further complications can arise if you then try to compensate for the injury. You will notice that professional athletes prepare their bodies for the demands they intend to place on them, warming muscles by stretching them through various light exercises. This is even more necessary for the nonprofessional whose body is not as conditioned.

Your preactivity stretching should be light: The object is to increase blood flow to those areas that will be under increased pressure to perform. Once the activity is finished you should stretch again to relax those muscles that may be bunched or shortened because of some particular use. As weightlifters have learned many repetitions will shorten and bulk-up muscles (it makes them appear more prominent) but slower exercises with their weights build strength. The longer you make the muscles through stretching the better their performance and less likely they are to be injured.

The muscles of some people are tighter than others. This is particularly true of older people and those under tension prior to the exercise. If your muscles are warmed up by stretching, they will perform more freely and will improve their coordination.

Testing Your Physical Fitness

You may ask yourself whether you need exercise and the answer is, of course, everyone does. But some need exercise more than others. How you might answer the question of how much is enough for you will vary depending upon your general health, your present fitness, and your physician's opinion.

The Step Test

A simple, but by no means comprehensive or conclusive, test of physical fitness is also an old one. Its principal appeal is that it can be conducted in your own home. During World War II the Harvard Fatigue Laboratories developed a test for college men purporting to measure the general capacity of the body to adapt itself to and recover from hard work. The test consists of observing pulse reaction to 5 minutes of stepping exercise. The test procedure is as follows:

Perform the stepping exercise on a twenty-inch bench or platform at the rate of thirty steps per minute for five minutes.

Each step involves four counts and the cadence of 120 counts per minute can be kept by counting aloud, "up, two, three, four," etc. Step up with one foot, then the other; step down with one foot, follow with the other. Your lead foot can be changed during the test, but no more than three times.

Following the completion of the exercise, sit down. After one minute take your pulse rate, taking a full minute's count. Your carotid pulse, below the ear, is recommended for this test.

The calculation score is derived by the formula: Index = Duration of exercise in seconds × 100 ÷ 5.5 × your pulse rate. Your score can be interpreted in broadest terms of general physical fitness: 50—poor; 50 to 80—average; and above 80—good.

For a slightly more detailed measure for the same exercise routine, upon completion sit down and count your pulse for thirty seconds, beginning at one minute, two minutes, and three minutes. The scoring then is done by this formula: Index = Duration of exercise in seconds × 100 ÷ 2 × sum of pulse rates in recovery.

If your thirty second pulse counts were 70, 65, and 60 (195), that sum multiplied by 2 (195 × 2 = 390) is to be divided into the number of seconds you performed the exercise multiplied by 100 (300 × 100 = 30,000). The computation is 30,000 ÷ 390 = 77). Fractions are discarded in using the formula.

The index or score is interpreted according to the following standards:

Below 55 . . . . . Poor physical condition
55 to 64 . . . . . Low average
65 to 74 . . . . . High average
75 to 84 . . . . . Good
Above 85 . . . . . Excellent

The Michigan Pulse Rate Test

Something called the Michigan Pulse Rate test for physical fitness was devised as a possible index of physical fitness that could be easily determined. The test is composed of (1) counting normal standing pulse; (2) performing a 15-second period of running in place at a rate of three steps per second; (3) counting standing pulse rate beginning ½, 1, 2, and 3 minutes after completion of the exercise; and (4) rating of your recovery time based on the following scale:

Time to recover normal	Grade	Fitness level
½ minute	A	Fine
1 minute	B	Good
2 minutes	C	Fair
3 minutes	D	Poor

These fitness tests were not designed to be very accurate or very comprehensive. They serve to begin rather than satisfy your questions of fitness. If you are seriously concerned about your endurance or stress fitness, there are stress tests that can measure the electrical activity of your heart, your pulse rate, blood pressure, and other indicators of any cardiovascular deficiencies while you go through a specific physical exercise. These stress tests are to be found in many hospitals and medical centers, and in "stress clinics" as well. However, once again, it is recommended that you consult your personal physician before you agree to any test whatsoever.

What a stress test can and should examine is your heart's strength and resilience to a measured amount of strain or effort. It determines this by its measure of your heart's ability to deliver oxygen-rich blood to your muscles as the test makes an increasing demand on them. This kind of exercise testing does not cure or improve your body's condition. Nor does it accurately determine any diagnosis of heart disease, whether the specific result of your test is negative or positive. But it can help predict the possibility of a future cardiovascular problem. It also can determine for you the safety of strenuous exercise even though you may show no signs of heart disease.

There are many excellent books available on the aerobic way of exercise. And they offer in detail convincing evidence of why you should live a life of exercise. But seeing, or in this instance doing, may be the real proof. For some students at the University of San Francisco it was just that.

Recent studies at the school established for a small group of students that aerobic exercise may be, after all, the best defense against their stress. The study involved a number of students in a fourteen-week program. The test group was selected from a sedentary group of students, not athletes as was often the case in earlier studies of the benefits of aerobic exercise. It was felt that temperamentally athletes were sufficiently different so that any studies citing their experiences through exercise would be less applicable to the general population.

The test group was divided in two. One was given a steady aerobic exercise program three to five times a week for approximately forty-five minutes to an hour. The other had no prescribed physical regimen. At the end of the study period both groups were given a variety of challenges including a set of unsolvable anagrams of which they all were told that the average college student could solve 80%. At the end of the test both groups were physically examined and the aerobic group had decidedly lower diastolic and systolic readings on their blood pressure including lower pulse rates than at the outset of the test. This was not true of the nonaerobic group.

The continuing growth of stimuli in our world of technological and social expansion, change and more change will make an increasing demand on our sympathetic nervous system. And it is the aerobic-exercised individual who will be able to withstand these growing stresses more successfully.

The simple fact is that regular aerobic physical exercise should be a part of everyone's life, no matter what their age; the overwhelming evidence, principally common sense, is an argument for a successful life of moderation. Less tension, less anger, less frustration, more comfort, more relaxation, more patience, less food, less weight, more energy, more work.

Chapter

6 Fuel For Stress

*What You Should Know
about the Relationship between
Nutrition and Stress*

Beware of Easy Nutritional Solutions

Nutritional misinformation can be found everywhere. Millions of dollars are spent on self-styled nutritional gurus and their worthless books, on monthly magazines, and especially on a wide range of products that claim nutritional schemes can prevent and cure ailments ranging from fatigue to cancer. Far too many people accept without question the testimonials of friends and acquaintances who believe they were helped by one or another nutrient, diet or food supplement.

The following questions are not designed to test what you do or do not know about nutrition. They are, rather, an introduction to nutrition by way of some vital facts that you should know, things most Americans know far too little about for their own good.

1. Recent clinical research demonstrates that "stress pills" or B-complex vitamins can be significantly effective in the reduction of stress in the otherwise healthy adult who is undergoing stress.   TRUE or FALSE.

2. The American diet is not only too high in carbohydrates but too low in protein.   TRUE or FALSE.

3. If unused by the body, large doses of vitamins such as A, D, E, and K may be expensive and wasteful but will be harmlessly washed out.   TRUE or FALSE.

4. There is no scientific evidence to support the fad that eating as many as six *light* meals a day (instead of three balanced meals of an equivalent amount of calories) can be the basis of a weight loss program.   TRUE or FALSE.

5. Despite what we learned from our parents, studies have shown that skipped breakfast, though not recommended, is *not* a health risk and neither is there any evidence that it increases the chance of an early death.   TRUE or FALSE.

6. Vitamin C is utilized at a higher rate in response to stress and therefore major doses should be taken to aid in stress tolerance.   TRUE or FALSE.

7. In an average balanced breakfast the total caloric intake should be 500-600, with protein contributing approximately 50%, fat 15-20%, and carbohydrates 30-35%.   TRUE or FALSE.

8. Only 10% of our food supply is unprocessed.   TRUE or FALSE.

9. Folic acid deficiency, which is the most common vitamin deficiency in the United States, is found most often in men over the age of forty-five.   TRUE or FALSE.

10. Despite the commercial promotion of iron supplements, a well-balanced diet usually protects the vast majority of American women from any iron deficiency.   TRUE or FALSE.

The correct answer to all these questions is FALSE. We will address each of the correct answers as we discuss the basic constituents of our diet, especially as they relate to stress.

Vitamins

One of the few vitamins that play a role in stress functions is vitamin C. Under stress it is possible that in some instances you may require a temporary increase but no more than 50% of the Recommended Daily Amount (RDA). The argument that massive doses of vitamin C is demanded during stress is simply not true. The adrenal glands can't accept more. Unless you are getting less C than the RDA as a general course of your daily diet, you will only waste your money on megadoses of vitamin C.

Some will argue that massive doses of vitamins have other salutary effects with no known adverse side effects. This is not always true. It is true that vitamin C is water soluble; it dissolves in water. Consequently it is not stored long term in your body, as excessive amounts taken are washed out of the body. Therefore if you are taking 100% or more than the RDA, given a balanced diet, you should drink two quarts of fluids each day, much of that preferably water. However, a dependency on megadoses of vitamin C can produce bladder and kidney stones, diarrhea and painful urinary-tract irritation. These are hardly salutary effects.

Vitamins A, D, E, and K are *not* water soluble. They are *fat* soluble and are stored for longer periods of time in the body. There is evidence that the prolonged use of major doses of such vitamins can be injurious. For example, excessive amounts of vitamin A can cause blurred vision, headaches, hair loss, menstrual irregularities, liver damage, and insomnia. A dramatic example of overdoing vitamin A concerned a Maine mother who followed the advice of the late Adelle Davis, and gave her daughter massive doses of A which permanently stunted the child's growth. According to Jane Brody of the *New York Times,* a damage suit against the Davis estate was settled out of court for $150,000. To avoid the hazards of vitamin A excesses, it is wisest to get your needed amount of A from your diet rather than from pills.

The prudent practice for the use of any vitamin is that if the body can't use it in the quantities you are giving it, you can't afford to use it.

Much has been said about the use of vitamins B_1 and B_{12} when under stress. However, there is no available clinical research evidence that warrants the use of megadoses of vitamins B_1 or B_{12} during stress conditions. It is true that vitamin B_1 (or thiamine) does help to release energy from your carbohydrates and assist in the synthesis of an important nervous-system chemical; and B_{12} also helps the functioning of your nervous system. But stress periods do not generally create the need for excessive use of these important vitamins. In fact, unless you are a strict vegetarian and therefore eat no animal flesh or their dairy products, you should not use large doses. A normally balanced diet should supply your needs. In fact, these vitamins are interdependent, so that an excess intake of any one may create a greater need for others. With the water-soluble vitamins, unused quantities are secreted in the urine. However, your motto always should be: *More is not only less, more can be another problem.*

Protein

Under *short-term stress* you should reduce your level of protein intake. Stress creates a build-up of a brain chemical called *norepinephrine,* produced from the protein in your body. The harmful role that norepinephrine plays is in producing acid. The more norepinephrine created, the more acidity we achieve. In fact, for more than ten years blood levels of norepinephrine have been a general indicator of stress. Consequently, during short periods of stress it is recommended that you reduce your intake of protein, particularly animal derived protein such as red meat and dairy products.

It is likely that you already consume too much protein in your diet. A healthy balanced diet need not contain any more than 12% protein; yet the average American has between 20% and 25% in his diet, and many eat as much as 40%. Unless you are eating a carbohydrate-deficient diet, the extra protein serves only as a source of additional calories, not energy.

Nutritionists generally recommend that no more than a third to a half of your protein needs should come from animal sources. The rest should come from vegetables. Regrettably most Americans rely on animal protein for 60% to 80% of their protein needs, protein rich in fat and cholesterol. Excessive amounts of animal protein will age your body although— ironically—the need for protein decreases as you grow older. Studies indicate that excessive animal protein intake can lead to stroke and other maladies, many provoked in part by excessive stress exposure.

If you reduce your protein intake you should increase your carbohydrates, particularly during short-term stress. This practice insures proper levels of energy, compensation for the reduced level of protein. Energy needs are often increased during stressful times, and fatigue often increases the stress and accompanying depression.

On the other hand, during *long-term stress* the body may

111

require the use of increased amounts of protein for its work. And serious protein loss is very dangerous. During a protracted period of stress, on an abnormally low-protein diet, protein loss can provoke both tissue loss and damage. Tissue loss is not uniform and therefore because of deficient amounts of available protein it can contribute not only to weight loss but, for example, the breakdown of heart tissue. Therefore, even though protein does produce norepinephrine, during periods of protracted stress your general health probably will require you to increase your protein intake, unless your protein intake is abnormally high already.

Breakfast

There are some risks involved in eating too quickly, in eating too much before going to bed at night, and in skipping breakfast. All are bad, but which is the worst? The *last* is probably the most important and the least observed.

Your first meal of the day occurs after at least an eight-hour fast, and if you eat early in the evening, as you should, the fast may be as long as twelve hours. A healthy body constantly maintains an appropriate blood sugar or glucose level so that you may have an energy supply readily available for your daily needs. To work efficiently, glucose levels must be maintained. However, after a night-long fast, your body will have to resupply the blood with glucose.

If it does not receive that nourishment in the form of a proper high-carbohydrate breakfast, it must and will draw upon the reserves it has stored in the liver. For the body to constantly withdraw its required amount of glucose from your liver each morning in the form of glycogen places undue stress on that organ.

Many individuals who have made a habit of skipping

breakfast claim they don't feel hungry that early in the day and that they don't experience any late morning periods of sluggishness or reduced efficiency. However, these people have almost no point of reference; they have no sense of what is possible, only of what they will settle for.

In fact, the habit of skipping or eating an inadequate breakfast can and does produce injurious results. Studies show that what you eat will affect your mood and performance. This is related to certain mechanisms in the body, such as those which regulate appetite, fluid and electrolyte balance, and neurotransmitter levels in the brain.

Fatigue is probably the most common excuse given for poor work performance, and nutritional deficiencies can contribute just as much to fatigue as the more apparent factors, such as inadequate rest or excessive work. Overall, poor eating habits diminish a person's abilities and can lead to exhaustion, apathy, poor concentration and reduced strength.

A study conducted by UCLA's Center for Health Science monitored approximately seven thousand men and women and it discovered that death rates were 40% *higher* for men and 28% *higher* for women who "rarely or sometimes" ate breakfast, compared with those who ate breakfast "almost every day." This evidence is likely to strike you as surprising, but irrelevent; as an adult you are the statistical exception. We can't predict whether you will actually suffer seriously from bad eating habits. We can, however, warn you that you place yourself in some *risk* by eating the inappropriate quantities of the wrong foods at the wrong times.

The gravity of the UCLA study is confirmed by a long-term study conducted by the University of Iowa which showed that eating a nutritious breakfast was associated with better physical and mental performance among children and adults. Those who ate breakfast were more productive and satisfied with their work performance during the late morning. Also, they had faster reaction times which, in many instances, resulted in fewer accidents on the job.

Another risk associated with skipping breakfast is that you are likely to miss some important nutrients, including vitamin C, thiamine (vitamin B₁), riboflavin (vitamin B₂), iron and calcium, nutrients that might be absent altogether in the other meals of the day. Only 5% of our food today is not processed in some manner, and processed food is notoriously low in essential nutrients. Eating one less meal a day only increases the odds that you will not consume all the essential nutrients.

Among adolescents who avoid a nutritious breakfast reports indicate that the calcium and vitamin C consumed during the remainder of the day is 40% less than among those who begin with a proper breakfast. The stress quotient is readily understood if your expected work or school performance is below the demand level. Furthermore it has been shown that the behavior of those who skip breakfast is to resort typically to coffee and sweet pastry, or snacks, when their stomach acids increase (causing hunger pains) and blood-sugar levels drop. However, the caffeine and refined or simple sugars they consume offer only short term relief. When these empty calories are exhausted the glucose level is brought back down, sharply.

Breakfast may seem to you as being like the opera; it is something you either go for or you don't. Often, though, the reason for not going for breakfast is just insufficient time. Evidence of that is the common practice of many weekday skippers of eating a generous weekend breakfast. Chapter 7 provides some shortcut nutritional "breakfast" ideas for those who don't have time every day.

More about Eating Habits

Ideally, the optimum eating schedule would be six light meals a day, equally spaced. They could represent six planned opportunities to take a rest-break from your schedule while, surprisingly, not creating a weight problem for yourself. The process of frequently secreting digestive juices utilizes energy; that energy is expended from the body in the form of lost heat and the process is referred to as *thermogenesis.* Therefore if you ate six meals (instead of the normal three) you would generate a heat loss twice as many times each day which could result in an actual loss of calories. It is not only conceivable but probable that through the practice of eating six meals (or some number greater than three) you would be able to actually consume more calories each day without any additional weight gain. It is equally possible that a weight loss could occur even with a small net gain in calories consumed.

Six meals a day would be impractical for most people. However, if you take time aside from your daily schedule to have "a small bite" as many people do, you can plan those meal-breaks to be nutritious (not the pit stop for coffee and a doughnut). This new and better eating pattern can be a more efficient way to fuel your system without storing greater reserves through excess.

Another advantage to multiple meals, of eating lighter and more frequently, is that the stomach can shrink to accommodate the bulk of the smaller meal. This assures that you will avoid the heaviness, the drugged drowsiness that often accompanies a heavy meal, to say nothing of the decided discomfort of flatulence or distension.

Calcium, Iron and Other Minerals

In some instances prolonged stress can produce mineral loss. One example is *calcium.*

Bones are commonly thought of as fixed, solid objects (containing 98% of the body's calcium), but in fact they continually lose and regain calcium. Furthermore, after the age of thirty-five calcium loss is greater than calcium gain. The amount reintroduced and absorbed does not equal that which is liberated. If calcium loss is severe, *osteoporosis* occurs, a progressive loss and weakening of bone density. Four percent of the female population beyond the age of menopause suffers from osteoporosis. However, calcium loss is not restricted to the older adult. Studies have revealed reduced bone density even in individuals as young as twenty-five. In total, probably 10 to 15% of all Americans have reduced bone density due to their inability to absorb and retain sufficient calcium in their bones.

If, after the age of thirty-five, the mineral loss remains unchecked, over the years it can advance and the bones can become brittle. Aside from a diet sufficient in vitamin D and calcium (provided by reasonable amounts of dairy products), the one recommended practice to retard this loss is *exercise.* Surprisingly, studies have shown that modest exercise programs of less than an hour, repeated three times a week, can slow or stop this loss. This is a particularly strong argument for every mature adult in our society to have a regular exercise program.

Should you increase your intake of one or more minerals by supplementary means outside the balanced diet? Probably not, since excessive increases can distort the physiological ratio between the various minerals, actually resulting in a deficiency of another mineral. For example, if you increased your intake of phosphorus through pills, or from the phosphates found in processed foods, your calcium will not be used efficiently.

Calcium absorption can be adversely affected by excessive dietary fat, and the consumption of large amounts of animal protein can result in an increased loss of calcium through the urine. A well-balanced diet and regular exercise is the best program and the safest way to meet the body's needs for balanced minerals.

The following chart lists those factors in your diet that can affect absorption of calcium, iron, folic acid, and zinc.

116

FACTORS AFFECTING ABSORPTION OF IRON, CALCIUM, FOLIC ACID AND ZINC

Nutrient	Absorption Enhanced by . . . . . . Found in	Absorption Decreased by . . . . . . Found in
Iron	Vitamin C . . . . citrus, tomatoes, cantaloupe, strawberries heme iron . . . . meats	Phylate* . . . . bran and germ of cereals (e.g. wheat, rice, corn, oats) tea . . . . commercial black and pekoe tea
Calcium	Vitamin D . . . . fish liver oils, fortified milk, salmon, (exposure to sunlight)	phytate . . . . (see above) oxalates . . . . spinach, cocoa and chocolate, beet greens, tea excess phosphorus . . . . . high meat diets
Zinc		phytate . . . . (see above) excess calcium . . . . (see Table 2)
Folic Acid	Glucose . . . . fruits, vegetables, grains	

*Cereals must comprise a high percentage of the diet to cause a significant reduction in available iron.

© 1981 Institute of Human Nutrition   College of Physicians and Surgeons   Columbia University   New York, N.Y.   All Rights Reserved

At the beginning of this chapter you answered a question about a vitamin called *folic acid*. Folic acid or *folacin* acts in concert with vitamin B_{12} and, according to the Institute of Human Nutrition, it is the most common vitamin deficiency, a deficiency found *most often* in women.

The reasons are varied. First, requirements increase during pregnancy because folic acid is needed for making new red blood cells so the fetus can grow properly. Second, if a woman is taking oral contraceptives, she is more prone to folic acid deficiency due to the known interference by the Pill with the *metabolism* of this vitamin. Furthermore, if she is a moderate to heavy drinker, she is at even greater risk because alcohol blocks the *absorption* of the vitamin.

FOLIC ACID CONTENT OF FOODS IN MICROGRAMS (mcg) PER SERVING

5-20 mcg/serving	20-50 mcg/servin g
carrot . . . . 1 med	green beans . . . . . 1 cup
ear of corn . . . . 1 med	cucumber . . . . 1 small
mushrooms . . . . . . 3 large	squash . . . . ⅔ cup
potato . . . . 1 med	strawberries . . . . . . 1 cup
apple . . . . 1 med	egg . . . . 1 large
hard cheese . . . . . 1 oz	kidney . . . . 3 oz
grapefruit . . . . ½ med	shellfish . . . . 6 oz
milk . . . . 8 oz	yogurt . . . . 8 oz
bread . . . . 1 slice	
sesame seeds . . . . 1 tbsp	
lean beef, veal or pork . . . . 6 oz	

100-150 mcg/serv ing	200-300 mcg/serv ing
liver (all) . . . . 3 oz	brewer's yeast . . . . 1 tbsp
broccoli . . . . 2 stalks	spinach . . . . 4 oz
orange juice . . . . . 6 oz	

Our diet contains very little folic acid, and women consuming limited numbers of calories, or those on diets which exclude those foods rich in folic acid are at risk.

The diet recommended especially for American women by the Institute of Human Nutrition is one that is rich in iron, calcium, folic acid, and zinc.

Zinc has been added to this list because it has been found recently that it is a fairly common deficiency, especially among pregnant women. While severe zinc deficiency does not often occur in the United States, mild deficiencies may be the cause of diminished appetite for some Americans and of poor growth patterns among the young. Nearly 60% of the land area in this country contains very little zinc, and this may account for the recent assumption about common deficiencies. The *New York Times* reported that otherwise healthy children in Denver were found to have impaired taste, poor appetite, and less than normal growth as a result of this deficiency. However, zinc is present in large amounts of food rich in iron.

Once again, it is advised that you do not take zinc (or iron) supplements without a physician's supervision. Excessive quantities can be troublesome. In fact, one 220 milligram capsule of zinc taken as a supplement can cause considerable discomfort, nausea, and vomiting.

Incidentally, the widespread promotion of iron supplements to the consumer market correctly points out the serious iron deficiency among American women. It is estimated that up to 30% of women have reduced iron stores and about 10% are anemic due to this deficiency. Women whose menstrual flow is heavy are more at risk than those who bleed lightly; and women who have had several pregnancies likewise are more at risk.

Some of the symptoms of the deficiencies are easy fatigue, weakness, and shortness of breath, not unlike those associated with heavy stress. Thus, it is recommended that all women should consume a diet rich in iron.

The following tables list foods rich in these four nutrients. Chapter 7 provides menu plans and meal ideas which emphasize these nutrients and which, for that reason, should be helpful to the average American woman.

This chapter and the one that follows are by no means comprehensive in their review of the dietary concerns that you should be aware of, whether at times of stress or anytime. You are encouraged to read more about the relationship between stress and nutrition. It is true: You *are* what you eat.

CALCIUM CONTENT OF FOODS

(Each portion provides approximately
300 mg of calcium)

Food	Amount
almonds	1 cup
amaranth	4 oz
broccoli	2¼ cups
cheese:	
cottage	12 oz
sandwich-style	1½ to 2 oz
custard	1 cup
fish (canned):*	
mackerel	3½ oz
salmon	5½ oz
sardines	3½ oz
ice cream (regular)	1⅔ cup
kelp	1½ oz
milk:	
whole, low-fat or	
buttermilk	8 oz
tofu (soybean curd)	8 oz
tortillas (6 in. diam.)	5
yeast (brewers)	14 tablespoons
yogurt	3/4-4/5 cup

*This calcium level includes the softened bones. If the bones are discarded the calcium content is greatly reduced.

© 1981 Institute of Human Nutrition   College of Physicians and Surgeons   Columbia University New York, N.Y.   All Rights Reserved

IRON CONTENT OF FOODS IN MILLIGRAMS (mg) PER SERVING

.3-.7 mg/serving

fruits: e.g., apples, bananas, cherries, melons, citrus, pineapple, etc.	avg. size
corn grits	1 cup
popcorn (popped)	1 cup
bread (all varieties)	1 slice
enriched macaroni, spaghetti or noodles	½ cup
peanut butter	2 tbsp
mushrooms	⅓ cup
eggplant	½ cup
tomato	1 small

2-4 mg/serving

amaranth	3½ oz
figs, dried	3 med
cooked peas & beans	½ cup
black strap molasses	1 tbsp
tofu (soybean curd)	4 oz

.7-1.4 mg/serving

rice, cooked (brown or white enriched)	1 cup
tortilla (6 in. diam.)	1
cream of wheat	1 cup
wheatena	⅔ cup
wheat germ	1 tbsp
dry bulgur wheat	2 tbsp
pumpkin seeds	1-2 tbsp
berries (all)	1 cup
broccoli	1 cup
carrots	1 cup
collards	1 cup
potato	1 med

4-5 mg/serving

beef (lean only), all cuts	3 oz
lamb (lean only), all cuts	4 oz
calf's liver	1 oz
raisins	½ cup

1.5-2 mg/serving

barley	½ cup
buckwheat	½ cup
oatmeal	1 cup
chicken (all cuts)	3-4 oz
bologna	3-4 oz
ham	2 oz
dried apricot halves	6 large
green beans	1 cup
brewer's yeast	1 tbsp

ZINC CONTENT OF FOODS IN MILLIGRAMS (mg) PER SERVING

.2 to .5 mg/serving

egg	1 med
gefilte fish	3½ oz
mango	½ med
applesauce	1 cup
pineapple juice	8 oz
tomato	1 med
potato, cooked	1 med

4 to 5 mg/serving

beef (lean only)	3½ oz
pork (lean only)	3½ oz
lamb (lean only)	3½ oz
liver (beef and calf)	3 oz

.5 to 1 mg/serving

puffed wheat	1 oz
cheddar cheese	1 oz
tuna	3 oz
white rice	1 cup
white bread	2 slices
cranberry-apple drink	8 oz
chicken breast	3 oz
milk (whole or skim)	8 oz

Other

9.4 mg Pacific oysters (raw)	3½ oz
74.7 mg Atlantic oysters (raw)	3½ oz

1 to 1.5 mg/serving

clams	3 oz
brown rice	1 cup
whole wheat bread	2 slices
popcorn	2 cups
wheat germ	1 tblsp
bran (cooked, dried)	¾ cup

© 1981 Institute of Human Nutrition   College of Physicians and Surgeons   Columbia University   New York, N.Y.   All Rights Reserved

Chapter

7 Starving Stress

Diets for the Stressful

Diet Modification

We know that there are many health risk areas in our lives which we simply cannot control. Advanced *age* and *heredity* are good examples. But the most easily controlled area of personal risk and probably the most important is *diet.* We are not talking merely of weight control, but rather of all the elements of a healthy diet, particularly those that reflect and meet your specific needs, including your emotional needs. Certain foods and certain diet patterns are fuel for stress, and *diet modification* is one of the most powerful tools every motivated and educated individual has to effect significant change towards improved health and reduced stress.

The more you understand the power you hold to assess your life critically and to understand the influences of various stimuli in your life, the happier, healthier and more successful you will be. Good health is not ever just a matter of being born with the right genes or being lucky; that certainly is not the case with regard to how and what you eat. There should be no doubt: *How you eat is what you become.* Diet does affect your mood and your performance.

Are you the typical American? Then you have probably had mixed results with diets. The most tempting, or initially promising, were those that offered the quickest results with the smallest effort. And while many of those programs were true to their claims, their results were passing. You only leased them; they were not for purchase. You found yourself eventually left with the same old problems, and—possibly—*new* problems.

The best diet programs are not those that result in dramatic weight loss in the shortest possible time. Long-term change in your daily eating habits takes time; your habits took time to become established and they will only reluctantly give up their hold over you. The changes must be made slowly, one day at a time. It is only cumulative and consecutive results, piled upon each other, that eventually will become permanent.

What is required absolutely is sensible diet planning, regimes that will appeal for a lifetime. Your program must take into account limited time resources, the entrenched attraction of older bad habits, and other inconveniences that can insidiously undermine your commitment and your goals.

Stress for Breakfast

You know already that breakfast is the most important and critical meal of the day. So start the day instead with a *good* breakfast. What is a good breakfast? Bacon, fried eggs, buttered toast, and coffee may taste good, but they are not ideal foods to choose. They constitute a high-fat meal, and a high-fat diet offers no advantage in starting your day. A good breakfast should average from three hundred to four hundred calories. The sample breakfasts that are offered below demonstrate how to distribute the calories in a nourishing and appealing way. Those calories generally should be distributed as follows: 50% as carbohydrates, 15 to 20% as protein, and 30 to 35% as fat.

Consuming more than 25% of your day's calories in the morning reduces overall efficiency. So it is not a large breakfast that is critical but a balanced or properly distributed meal. In this light there is nothing wrong with an unorthodox breakfast—leftovers—if it meets the requirements of a good breakfast.

If you find that breakfast is a bore or that your family resists the traditional idea of breakfast a little imagination may be required to satisfy nutritional needs. Try the following changes:

- *Toast* to chicken wings or sweet potatoes stuffed with cottage cheese sprinkled with wheat germ
- *Eggs* to rice
- *Ham* to orange sections or pineapple chunks
- *Coffee* to herb tea or molasses drink

Even if breakfast is eaten after leaving home, try to get to it at the first possible opportunity. A can of vegetable juice, a bag of peanuts (preferably unsalted), a package of raisins, with hot chocolate from a vending machine, is a temporary but tolerable substitute.

If it is your practice to put a raw egg in with other ingredients to make a shake as a high-potency morning drink, *don't!* Raw eggs contain a substance, *avidin,* which will bind to the vitamin *biotin* and make it unavailable for your body's use.

125

Cooking the egg renders the avidin harmless, though it is not recommended that the cooked egg be placed in the shake. If you, or some members of your family, like these shakes for breakfast, add one or two tablespoons of nonfat dry milk, yogurt, or fruit juice, and blend until frothy.

Break-Time

Besides something to give you a lift in the morning, to get you started, you need to avoid that mid-morning slump that many people treat with empty calories such as coffee and pastry. One procedure I urge you to try should be done even before breakfast: a brief period of exercise or stretching. It need not be strenuous or time consuming. Five minutes of stretching exercises, such as a modified yoga program, provides a sense of well-being and energy that is superior to caffeine.

While on the subject of coffee, it can contribute to mid-morning sluggishness. If you are a heavy coffee drinker, try tea which has as little as half the caffeine of regular coffee, or at least cut the coffee with decaffeinated. Incidentally, though you may feel you do not experience any adverse side effects from caffeine, it is nevertheless likely that your tolerance for irritable situations, calling for greater patience, will improve with less coffee consumption in the morning. Furthermore, it is a medical fact that coffee consumption in excess of eight cups increases the likelihood of bio-cystic breast disease, low-grade fevers, and other unpleasant side effects. Caffeine may seem commonplace, but it *is* a drug and can be abused.

It has been observed that it is not the coffee or pastry in the coffee break that is desired so much as the break or pause from the work schedule. The following is a table that describes the usual items eaten at the coffee break and proposes some alternatives that can lead you to better habits.

126

REVISING THE REFRESHMENT BREAK

Item	Reason for Omitting	Alternative
coffee & tea	caffeine = gastric distress	caffeine-free coffee & teas, herb teas, fruit juices
soft drinks	high in caffeine & sugar	
sugar & saccharin	low nutrient density linked to cancer	cinnamon
cream & coffee lighteners	high in saturated fat	skimmed, evaporated milk
lemon juice	(none)	(none)
whole milk	high in saturated fat	low fat milk
cocoa	high in sugar	low sugar varieties
pastries	high in sugar & saturated fat	low fat muffins, raisin bread
candy bars	high in sugar & saturated fat	fresh or dried fruit

If you determine it is refreshment that you want at this break-time consider the following: First, there is no rule that says you have to eat just because it's break-time. After giving it some thought you may conclude that what you really want is some stimulation *or* relaxation; therefore it is advised that you either try simple stretching or breathing exercises, perhaps the same ones with which you started the day, or the brief relaxation exercise we covered in Chapter 4. Secondly, water is an often omitted but very important element in a good diet. It refreshes and flushes the body's systems. To break into the water habit substitute a glass of water for one of the cups of coffee or other beverages you might have during the break-time.

If you are at home or can bring a prepared snack to your workplace, try a mid-morning snack of plain yogurt and a slice of whole-grain bread. Whether or not your breakfast includes any foods rich in vitamin C, you still can have fresh fruit or a glass of tomato juice, very important foods in any stress diet.

Specific Prescriptions for Stress

During the course of your day or week, stress exposure may naturally increase due to some predictable events, pleasant or unpleasant. In most instances there is no evidence for the need for megadoses of vitamins even under stress when certain physiological changes occur: It is protein consumption during short- and long-term stress periods that requires careful watching.

For example, during extended periods of stress proper protein levels should be maintained; therefore your diet should include several protein-rich foods. If your breakfast contained low-fat milk or yogurt, your second main meal might include eggs, and the evening meal fish or poultry, such as breast of turkey.

It's possible that stress levels interrupt the effective metabolism of B-vitamins; thus it is a suitable precaution that you incorporate whole grain foods in your stress diet. Items like rice in the evening and whole-grain bread or bran cereals should be staples in your diet planning.

During stress you may experience gastrointestinal distress, particularly gas. If so, you should reduce the amount of food at any one sitting and increase the occasions for eating. Your digestive tract may not completely digest all of the carbohydrates of a major meal; in combination with certain other foods, such as beans and broccoli that provide necessary intestinal bacteria, gas will result. Eating too quickly during stress will only aggravate the problem by slowing the digestive process and generating pockets of painful or embarrassing gas.

Swallowed air is thought to be the primary cause of excessive gas. If you are anxious or stressful you may take in too much air while eating. When your mother admonished you about talking with your mouth full she was also, though perhaps unwittingly, preventing a practice that can emit excessive and troublesome air. If you suffer from gas during periods of stress it is recommended that you don't chew gum, suck on candies, or consume carbonated beverages. The first two add more swallowed air, and the latter introduces additional carbon dioxide into your stomach that must eventually escape.

Eating properly may not prevent stress, but it certainly can prevent some of the physical discomforts associated with it. You know your energy level must be maintained to steady your nerves and avoid stress-related fatigue. Consequently, watch what you eat. Plan meals not only for convenience but to ensure that they meet the emotional needs of you and your family. Be aware of eating habits as contributors to food-related problems. Finally, if you are taking any medication, which almost always involves some stress, take some effort to learn how they affect the foods you normally eat. The use of drugs can alter the manner in which your body handles essential nutrients. Anyone who has special nutritional requirements and consumes a number of medications is at potential risk for drug-induced nutrient deficiencies.

To offset any known losses due to drug-nutritional interaction it is advised that one consume at least two extra servings per day of the foods that are high in those nutrients that are affected. For reference, the following table is a list of commonly taken drugs which can cause alterations in your metabolism.

FOOD SOURCES OF NUTRIENTS COMMONLY AFFECTED BY DRUGS

NUTRIENT	FOOD SOURCES
Vitamin A	Liver, butter, cream, egg yolks, leafy green vegetables, deep yellow and orange fruits and vegetables
B Vitamins Folic Acid	Liver, yeast, leafy green vegetables, legumes, whole grains, fruits and other vegetables
B^6	Wheat germ, meat, liver, whole grains, peanuts, soybeans, corn
B^{12}	Liver, eggs, meat, milk, cheese
Vitamin C	Citrus fruits, strawberries, tomatoes, cantaloupes, broccoli, cabbage, green peppers, leafy greens, potatoes
Vitamin D	Fish liver oils, fortified milks, very small amounts in egg yolks, butter, liver, salmon, sardines
Vitamin K	Leafy green vegetables, liver
Calcium	Milk, cheese, leafy green vegetables, clams, oysters, almonds, legumes, water, tofu
Iron	Liver, meat, oysters, leafy green vegetables, dried apricots, prunes, peaches, raisins, legumes, nuts, whole grains
Magnesium Phosphorus	Whole grains, legumes, nuts, leafy green vegetables, water Liver, meat, eggs, milk, cheese, nuts, legumes, whole grains, refined cereals
Potassium	Meat, milk, leafy green vegetables, dates, bananas, canta-loupes, apricots, citrus fruits, bamboo shoots, prunes
Zinc	Oysters, liver, wheat germ, yeast, seafood

AFTERWORD

We have talked at length about how stress can adversely affect your good health, and how good health can also be the best defense.

While the book has been focused ostensibly on stress, taken in a broader perspective it is also about the powers which reside in you to critically assess yourself, to recognize and be sensitive to the multitude and variety of stimuli that constantly assault you, to understand their effect, and ultimately to control their influence.

In short, *Personal Strategies* can be viewed as a book about change.

No one achieves successful changes, however, by the mere exercise of will. In order to modify your behavior to improve your health significantly, you need more than strong motivation or simple determination. You need a heightened awareness; you must set realistic goals and limits; you must be committed. All essential requirements if you are to succeed in harnessing your innate powers to produce more positive change in your life.

131

The behaviors that are most troublesome in your life probably are those that escape your self-control, those that are compulsive. If you suffer from some seemingly intractable behaviors that have resisted earlier change efforts, consider the following:

● Keep a private behavior-diary or journal. It is likely that your memory serves to support your present behavior; it is only selectively honest. The truly honest written record usually uncovers that which unconsciously wants to remain covered. For example, a written inventory can reveal the antecedent cues (those events or feelings that precede and possibly influence the behavior) of which you are not fully aware.

● Develop a plan or strategy to deal with these identified antecedent cues. If one of the antecedent feelings is anxiety or depression which you treat with alcohol, develop another problem-free response, such as a relaxation exercise. The antecedent cues discovered through self-awareness record-keeping may be the real problems and not your inadequate response to them.

● Resist or delay your compelling and predictable reaction to your antecedent cue as long as possible. It will slowly begin to lose its hold over you. A "thought-stopping" technique is a good example of how to take the initiative on a situation that only seems to own your will.

For every craving there are usually a variety of possible responses. In many instances we just choose the wrong one, or the only one. If you don't learn to have an alternative, pro-active Plan B (or Plan C, for that matter) you will always be a captive of your no-choice, re-active Plan A. Also, your alternatives should have elements of support so that they are as attractive as the compulsive Plan A.

Any smoker can quite smoking—and most have, many times. Constant self-watching and self-managing is the key to consolidating and preserving your successes. Most relapses grow out of an inability to anticipate a problem; they occur when your conscious defenses are down. Therefore, you must never forget. Your strategy must contain the elements of "I never do that anymore," "I don't have to do that anymore" as well as "I enjoy *this* now."

Being aware constantly of what you have left behind renews your commitment and reminds you of the quiet threat an old compulsion can have. If you are to continue in your new behavior, you require continuous self-examination. You need to record your behavior without self-editing. It is *for your eyes only.*

Simply having more information does not insure that you will change. Simply knowing the negative consequence of not changing does not insure that you will avoid them. Planned change occurs reluctantly, because there are some powerful interests opposed to them.

One effective way of seeing the resistance you may face in a specific change effort is through a *force-field analysis.* Force-field analysis is a powerful idea intrinsically related to all personal efforts to change behavior. It is a crucial aspect of assessment which permits you to understand the entire context in which your change will occur.

The following is a model of how you might construct your own analysis:

1. What are the things which can help you right now to make changes you desire? List them.
2. What are the things which may hold you back from achieving your desired goals to change? List them.
3. How can you increase a motivating force?
4. How can you *decrease* a restraining force?

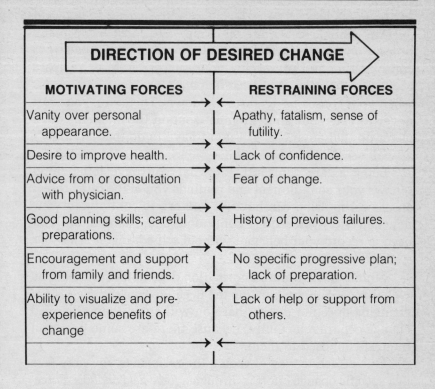

DIRECTION OF DESIRED CHANGE	
MOTIVATING FORCES	**RESTRAINING FORCES**
Vanity over personal appearance.	Apathy, fatalism, sense of futility.
Desire to improve health.	Lack of confidence.
Advice from or consultation with physician.	Fear of change.
Good planning skills; careful preparations.	History of previous failures.
Encouragement and support from family and friends.	No specific progressive plan; lack of preparation.
Ability to visualize and pre-experience benefits of change	Lack of help or support from others.

Conflicting forces may lead to discouragement or total inertia, no matter how strongly change may be desired. But it may be far easier for you to move towards the desired change by eliminating or reducing just one restraining force. Certainly they will not all go away.

Pushing harder, adding additional motivating force, may succeed in increased resistance from restraining forces. But reducing the number or degree of forces holding you back may tip the balance in your favor, and make success easier to achieve.

The support of others is most often the strongest motivating force in any one individual's ability to change. Conversely, isolation (the absence of support) can be the strongest restraining force.

134

Many successful changes are brought about through the support of *groups*: family members, peer groups, support group organizations (e.g., A.A., Smokenders, Weight Watchers, etc.), whereas few meaningful changes occur easily for the individual who is cut off from the support of others.

To best insure success in achieving your goal for change, it is essential to assess *all of the forces* which may impact upon your ability to bring about change, both the positive motivating forces and the negative restraining forces.

If you have difficulty identifying a specific change you want to attempt or making a patient systematic preparation for it, try the following exercise.

1. Begin by compiling a list of all the things you already do that promote fitness and good health.

    Examples: a. I do isometric exercises 15 minutes every day.

    b. I limit myself to one glass of wine at lunch.

    c. I take long, brisk walks and I jog 3-4 miles every Saturday and Sunday.

2. Now compile a *second* list of behaviors you'd like to change or eliminate, and specific areas you'd like to improve.

    Examples: a. I usually skip breakfast, and I tend to eat impulsively and erratically.

    b. I frequently have lower back pain, and I do no exercise to improve this condition.

    c. I smoke a pack of cigarettes a day, and I have never been able to quit.

3. Select *one* pattern of behavior from the second list that you'd like to work on and improve. Now plan to *change your behavior:*

       a. List all the *positive* effects of changing that behavior;

       b. Now list all the *negative* effects of *not* changing that behavior.

4. Visualize yourself engaging in your new, improved behavior. *Concentrate!* This is an effort to break the boundaries of time so that you can "witness" the future benefits of a decision being made *now*. Visualize—in as much detail as possible—the benefits which will accrue to you in two, three weeks. . .six months from now. . .!

5. Build *a support system* for your self-directed change in behavior:

       a. *Find a partner* who will agree to participate in or review your plan, and who will support you in achieving your goal. What specifically can a partner *do* to help support your plan?

       b. Plan on how you will *reward yourself* when you've achieved your goal. Look forward to that reward; remind yourself of it frequently; make it a real treat, one worth struggling for.

6. *Evaluate your plan:*

       a. How will you keep track of your progress?

       b. How often will you assess your progress?

       c. What will you do if progressive improvement is not occurring on schedule?

       d. *Revise your plan* if it is not realistic.

7. Complete the CHECKLIST FOR CHANGE:

__ I'm working on the health area I most want to improve, and which I believe I can do the most about.

__ I can identify the specific behavior which needs to be changed, and I know why it occurs.

__ I know what I enjoy about that behavior, and why it still exists.

__ I have listed all the positive benefits of changing that behavior.

__ I have listed all the negative consequences of *not* changing that behavior.

__ I have a clear plan and realistic goals for changing that behavior.

__ I can visualize the benefits of this new, improved behavior beginning to occur in the not-too-distant future.

__ I have identified the specific steps I need to take to achieve my goal.

__ I have a partner to support me in my efforts. This person has agreed to play a specific role to help me evaluate progress and achieve my goal.

__ I have planned a specific reward for myself when I achieve my goal, and I look forward to earning my reward.

__ I have developed a simple system for keeping track of my progress.

__ I have set a specific time to evaluate my progress, and to revise my plan as needed. My partner has agreed to help me with this evaluation.

If you are not able to check everything on the CHECKLIST FOR CHANGE, you may have a weakness in your preparation that requires your attention before beginning. It is not so important to begin but to finish.

Too many of us want change but fail to prepare for it. Too often we do not plan carefully when we desire change. Your careful planning need not be complicated, just thought through. Your preparation should provide the confidence needed to see the effort through to a successful completion because you understand what is to be accomplished, and why, and you have identifed and assembled the necessary resources to assist you.

Real change occurs when the individual being changed is the very instrument of that change. *You!*

Note to the reader:
On the following pages is a copy of both the FILE and PROFILE with a Computation Scale and Comparison Graphs for your personal use.

PROFILES

INSTRUCTIONS

Please fill in the circles that best describe your experiences.

(Part 1) Please identify how often each of the following events occur in your home life or work setting.

3 = Often   2 = Sometimes   1 = Rarely   0 = Never

(Part 2) When the following situations occur, how much stress or impact does each have on your functioning at home or on the job.

3 = Major Effect   2 = Some Effect   1 = No Effect

Check *DOES NOT APPLY(✓)* if the statement is not possible for you.

WORK AND FAMILY CONFLICT ISSUES

	PART 1 How Often? Often ③ Sometimes ② Rarely ① Never ⓪	Apply Not Apply	PART 2 How Affected? Major Effect ③ Some Effect ② No Effect ①
	(fill in one circle) ③ ② ① ⓪	✓	(fill in one) ③ ② ①
A1 My work schedule creates problems for me	③ ② ① ⓪		③ ② ①
B1 Distance to my job creates problems for me	③ ② ① ⓪		③ ② ①

Code	Statement		
C1	Getting a promotion is a problem where I work	③ ② ① ⓪	③ ② ①
E1	Problems getting along with customers or clients	③ ② ① ⓪	③ ② ①
G1	Children's personal problems need my attention	③ ② ① ⓪	③ ② ①
K1	Anger or tense relations lead to bad work atmosphere	③ ② ① ⓪	③ ② ①
M1	Too tired to do things with family when get home	③ ② ① ⓪	③ ② ①
N1	Scheduling adequate child care is difficult	③ ② ① ⓪	③ ② ①
P1	Family does not support or approve of job	③ ② ① ⓪	③ ② ①
B2	Problems due to changing job site or location	③ ② ① ⓪	③ ② ①
D1	Work conditions are uncomfortable or distracting	③ ② ① ⓪	③ ② ①
F1	My job is not everything I wanted it to be	③ ② ① ⓪	③ ② ①
H1	Marital difficulties are a source of concern	③ ② ① ⓪	③ ② ①
I1	Problems with family financial matters	③ ② ① ⓪	③ ② ①
J1	Too tired or not physically ready when go to work	③ ② ① ⓪	③ ② ①
M2	Nervous, tense or frustrated when get home	③ ② ① ⓪	③ ② ①
O1	Family is neglected and not as close as it could be	③ ② ① ⓪	③ ② ①
A2	Long working hours are a problem for me	③ ② ① ⓪	③ ② ①

WORK AND FAMILY CONFLICT ISSUES

		PART 1 — How Often? (fill in one circle) Often(3) Sometimes(2) Rarely(1) Never(0)	Apply / Not Apply	PART 2 — How Affected? (fill in one) Major Effect(3) Some Effect(2) No Effect(1)
C2	Employer policy on payment of wages creates problems	③ ② ① ⓪		③ ② ①
F2	My employer demands too much from my job	③ ② ① ⓪		③ ② ①
H2	Problems with parent-child relationships	③ ② ① ⓪		③ ② ①
J2	Loss of time at work because of other problems	③ ② ① ⓪		③ ② ①
M3	My personal health is a problem	③ ② ① ⓪		③ ② ①
O2	Hard to find enough time to be alone with spouse	③ ② ① ⓪		③ ② ①
B3	The place I work is in a dangerous location	③ ② ① ⓪		③ ② ①
E2	Trouble getting along with my employer	③ ② ① ⓪		③ ② ①
G2	My spouses' personality creates problems	③ ② ① ⓪		③ ② ①
J3	Personal concerns reduce my productivity at work	③ ② ① ⓪		③ ② ①

Code	Statement							
M4	My health and satisfaction are affected by problems	③ ② ① ⓪			③ ② ①
P2	Family disagreements about things related to work	③ ② ① ⓪			③ ② ①
C3	Salary and benefits of my job creates problems	③ ② ① ⓪			③ ② ①
F3	Some things about my job are a problem for me	③ ② ① ⓪			③ ② ①
I2	Lack resources to meet family's desired lifestyle	③ ② ① ⓪			③ ② ①
L1	Home duties are unfinished or not done very well	③ ② ① ⓪			③ ② ①
O3	Family members are irritable or tense at home	③ ② ① ⓪			③ ② ①
C4	My pay is unfair or not enough	③ ② ① ⓪			③ ② ①
F4	Type of job I have creates problems for me	③ ② ① ⓪			③ ② ①
I3	My lifestyle and personal interests lead to problems	③ ② ① ⓪			③ ② ①
N2	Family needs and activities are hard to schedule	③ ② ① ⓪			③ ② ①
A3	Can never be sure what hours I will work	③ ② ① ⓪			③ ② ①
E3	Trouble getting along with some of my co-workers	③ ② ① ⓪			③ ② ①
I4	Difficulties caused by friends or relatives	③ ② ① ⓪			③ ② ①
M5	Feel guilty about neglect of family	③ ② ① ⓪			③ ② ①
A4	Having no control over work hours is a problem	③ ② ① ⓪			③ ② ①
D2	Work situation is dangerous or unsafe	③ ② ① ⓪			③ ② ①
G3	My personality or personal habits create problems	③ ② ① ⓪			③ ② ①

WORK AND FAMILY CONFLICT ISSUES

		PART 1		PART 2
		How Often? Often ③ Sometimes ③ Rarely ① Never ⓪ (fill in one circle)	Apply Not Apply	How Affected? Major Effect ③ Some Effect ③ No Effect ① (fill in one)
J4	Other commitments interfere with my work performance	③ ② ① ⓪		③ ② ①
L2	Not taking time to do extra things around house	③ ② ① ⓪		③ ② ①
P3	Disagree on whether should be at work or with family	③ ② ① ⓪		③ ② ①
C5	My employee benefits are not enough for my needs	③ ② ① ⓪		③ ② ①
G4	Family member personal problems create difficulties	③ ② ① ⓪		③ ② ①
J5	Problems concentrating on my job when at work	③ ② ① ⓪		③ ② ①
N3	Community or school meetings are hard to attend	③ ② ① ⓪		③ ② ①
P4	Disagree with spouse on need for both of us to work	③ ② ① ⓪		③ ② ①
F5	My job is demanding, tedious and/or too tense	③ ② ① ⓪		③ ② ①
K2	Not interested in or happy about my job	③ ② ① ⓪		③ ② ①

Code	Item		
O4	Family satisfaction is less due to other problems	③ ② ① ⓪	③ ② ①
E4	Problems getting along with some people at work	③ ② ① ⓪	③ ② ①
I5	Problems created by trying to schedule family needs	③ ② ① ⓪	③ ② ①
P5	Concern about what spouse does while at their job	③ ② ① ⓪	③ ② ①
D3	Working conditions at my job are a problem	③ ② ① ⓪	③ ② ①
H3	Marriage or family matters create problems for me	③ ② ① ⓪	③ ② ①
N4	Family health checkups or exercise hard to set up	③ ② ① ⓪	③ ② ①
B4	My job is located in an undesirable place	③ ② ① ⓪	③ ② ①
H4	Family problems are a source of concern	③ ② ① ⓪	③ ② ①
K3	Trouble with co-workers causes bad work situation	③ ② ① ⓪	③ ② ①
L3	Hard to complete household duties when tired or busy	③ ② ① ⓪	③ ② ①
E5	Supervisor on my job creates problems for me	③ ② ① ⓪	③ ② ①
N5	Difficult to schedule recreational activities	③ ② ① ⓪	③ ② ①
H5	Concern about children fighting with each other	③ ② ① ⓪	③ ② ①
B5	Location of my job leads to certain problems	③ ② ① ⓪	③ ② ①

FILE

FAMILY INVENTORY OF LIFE EVENTS AND CHANGES

Hamilton I. McCubbin   Joan M. Patterson

Purpose

Over their life cycle, all families experience many changes as a result of normal growth and development of members and due to external circumstances. The following list of family life changes can happen in a family at any time. Because family members are connected to each other in some way, a life change for any one member affects all the other persons in the family to some degree.

"FAMILY" means a group of two or more persons living together who are related by blood, marriage or adoption. This includes persons who live with you *and* to whom you have a long term commitment.

Directions

"DID THE CHANGE HAPPEN IN YOUR FAMILY?"

Please read each family life change and decide whether it happened to any member of your family—including you.

● DURING THE LAST YEAR
First, decide if it happened any time during the last 12 months and check the appropriate box. If the answer is YES, enter the score.

Yes	No	Score
☐	46 ☐	☐

FAMILY LIFE CHANGES

	DID THE CHANGE HAPPEN IN YOUR FAMILY? During Last 12 Mo.		
	Yes	No	Score
I. INTRA-FAMILY STRAINS			
1. Increase of husband father's time away from family	☐	☐	46
2. Increase of wife mother's time away from family	☐	☐	51
3. A member appears to have emotional problems	☐	☐	58
4. A member appears to depend on alcohol or drugs	☐	☐	66
5. Increase in conflict between husband and wife	☐	☐	53
6. Increase in arguments between parent(s) and child(ren)	☐	☐	45
7. Increase in conflict among children in the family	☐	☐	48
8. Increased difficulty in managing teenage child(ren)	☐	☐	55
9. Increased difficulty in managing school age child(ren) (6–12 yrs.)	☐	☐	39
10. Increased difficulty in managing preschool age child(ren) (2–6 yrs.)	☐	☐	36
11. Increased difficulty in managing toddler(s) (1–2 yrs.)	☐	☐	36
12. Increased difficulty in managing infant(s) (0–1 yrs.)	☐	☐	35
13. Increase in the amount of "outside activities" which the child(ren) are involved in	☐	☐	25
14. Increased disagreement about a member's friends or activities	☐	☐	35
15. Increase in the number of problems or issues which don't get resolved	☐	☐	43
16. Increase in the number of tasks or chores which don't get done	☐	☐	35
17. Increased conflict with in-laws or relatives	☐	☐	40
II. MARITAL STRAINS			
18. Spouse/parent was separated or divorced	☐	☐	79
19. Spouse/parent has an "affair"	☐	☐	68
20. Increased difficulty in resolving issues with a "former" or separated spouse	☐	☐	47

FAMILY LIFE CHANGES

No.	Family Life Change	DID THE CHANGE HAPPEN IN YOUR FAMILY? During Last 12 Mo. Yes	No	Score
21.	Increased difficulty with sexual relationship between husband and wife	☐	☐	58
III. PREGNANCY AND CHILDBEARING STRAINS				
22.	Spouse had unwanted or difficult pregnancy	☐	☐	45
23.	An unmarried member became pregnant	☐	☐	65
24.	A member had an abortion	☐	☐	50
25.	A member gave birth to or adopted a child	☐	☐	50
IV. FINANCE AND BUSINESS STRAINS				
26.	Took out a loan or refinanced a loan to cover increased expenses	☐	☐	29
27.	Went on welfare	☐	☐	55
28.	Change in conditions (economic, political, weather) which hurts the family business	☐	☐	41
29.	Change in Agriculture Market, Stock Market, or Land Values which hurts family investments and or income	☐	☐	43

FAMILY LIFE CHANGES

No.	Family Life Change	DID THE CHANGE HAPPEN IN YOUR FAMILY? During Last 12 Mo. Yes	No	Score
43.	Decrease in satisfaction with job/career	☐	☐	45
44.	A member had increased difficulty with people at work	☐	☐	32
45.	A member was promoted at work or given more responsibilities	☐	☐	40
46.	Family moved to a new home/apartment	☐	☐	43
47.	A child adolescent member changed to a new school	☐	☐	24
VI. ILLNESS AND FAMILY "CARE" STRAINS				
48.	Parent/spouse became seriously ill or injured	☐	☐	44
49.	Child became seriously ill or injured	☐	☐	35
50.	Close relative or friend of the family became seriously ill	☐	☐	44
51.	A member became physically disabled or chronically ill	☐	☐	73
52.	Increased difficulty in managing a chronically ill or disabled member	☐	☐	58

No.	Item	Value
30.	A member started a new business	50
31.	Purchased or built a home	41
32.	A member purchased a car or other major item	19
33.	Increasing financial debts due to over-use of credit cards	31
34.	Increased strain on family "money" for medical/dental expenses	23
35.	Increased strain on family "money" for food, clothing, energy, home care	21
36.	Increased strain on family "money" for child(ren)'s education	22
37.	Delay in receiving child support or alimony payments	41

V. WORK-FAMILY TRANSITIONS AND STRAINS

No.	Item	Value
38.	A member changed to a new job/career	40
39.	A member lost or quit a job	55
40.	A member retired from work	48
41.	A member started or returned to work	41
42.	A member stopped working for extended period (e.g., laid off, leave of absence, strike)	51
53.	Member or close relative was committed to an institution or nursing home	44
54.	Increased responsibility to provide direct care or financial help to husband's and/or wife's parent(s)	47
55.	Experienced difficulty in arranging for satisfactory child care	40

VII. LOSSES

No.	Item	Value
56.	A parent/spouse died	98
57.	A child member died	99
58.	Death of husband's or wife's parent or close relative	48
59.	Close friend of the family died	47
60.	Married son or daughter was separated or divorced	58
61.	A member "broke up" a relationship with a close friend	35

VIII. TRANSITIONS "IN AND OUT"

No.	Item	Value
62.	A member was married	42
63.	Young adult member left home	43
64.	A young adult member began college (or post high school training)	28

FAMILY LIFE CHANGES

FAMILY LIFE CHANGES	DID THE CHANGE HAPPEN IN YOUR FAMILY? During Last 12 Mo.		
	Yes	No	Score
65. A member moved back home or a new person moved into the household	☐	42 ☐	☐
66. A parent/spouse started school (or training program) after being away from school for a long time	☐	38 ☐	☐
IX. FAMILY LEGAL VIOLATIONS			
67. A member went to jail or juvenile detention	☐	68 ☐	☐

FAMILY LIFE CHANGES	DID THE CHANGE HAPPEN IN YOUR FAMILY? During Last 12 Mo.		
	Yes	No	Score
68. A member was picked up by police or arrested	☐	57 ☐	☐
69. Physical or sexual abuse or violence in the home	☐	75 ☐	☐
70. A member ran away from home	☐	61 ☐	☐
71. A member dropped out of school or was suspended from school	☐	38 ☐	☐
Total FILE score			☐

When you complete your total(s) consult the TABLE on page 17 to compare your family score with the norms for your particular Family Stage.

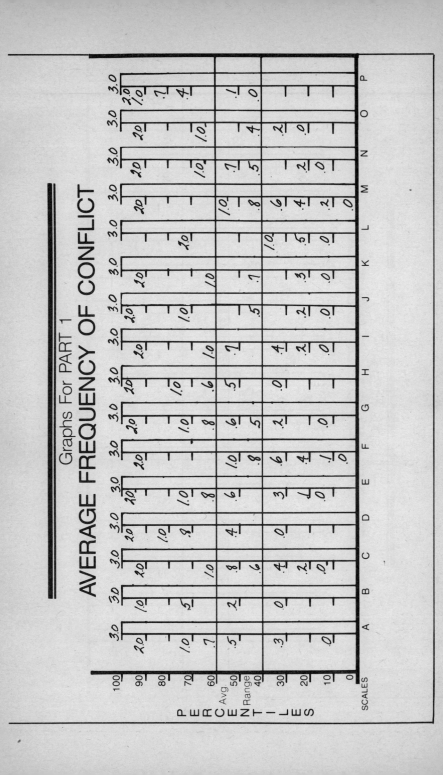

Graphs For PART 1

AVERAGE FREQUENCY OF CONFLICT

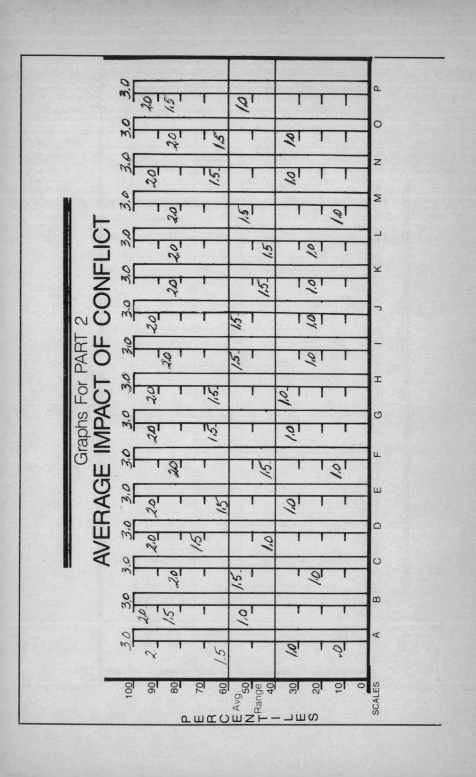

Graphs For PART 2

AVERAGE IMPACT OF CONFLICT

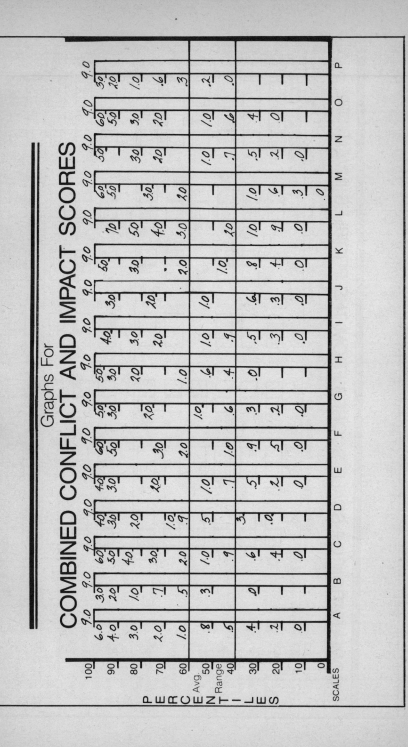

Graphs For
COMBINED CONFLICT AND IMPACT SCORES

COMPUTATION OF SCALE SCORES FROM THE PROFILES INVENTORY

Part 1 = How Often
Part 2 = Effect

PROFILES Scale Titles	Addition of Items in Each Scale (Part 1 / Part 2)	Raw Score Totals	Divided By # of Items (Part 1 / Part 2)	Average Scores	Combined Conflict And Impact Score (Graph These Scores) Conflict / Impact / Combined

PROBLEMS ASSOCIATED WITH WORK

Scale	Items	Raw	Divided	Average
Work Schedules — Scale A	$A_1 + A_2 + A_3 + A_4 = A_5$	$= A$	$\div 4 =$	
Job Location — Scale B	$B_1 + B_2 + B_3 + B_4 = B_5$	$= B$	$\div 5 =$	
Salary & Benefits — Scale C	$C_1 + C_2 + C_3 + C_4 = C_5$	$= C$	$5 =$	
Work Environment — Scale D	$D_1 + D_2 + D_3 +$	$= D$	$3 =$	
Work Relationships — Scale E	$E_1 + E_2 + E_3 + E_4 = E_5$	$= E$	$5 =$	
Job Characteristics — Scale F	$F_1 + F_2 + F_3 + F_4 = F_5$	$= F$	$5 =$	

PROBLEMS ASSOCIATED WITH FAMILY

Scale	Items	Raw	Divided	Average
Personal Problems — Scale G	$G_1 + G_2 + G_3 + G_4 = G_4$	$= G$	$4 =$	
Interpersonal Problems — Scale H	$H_1 + H_2 + H_3 + H_4 = H_5$	$= H$	$5 =$	
Family Environment — Scale I	$I_1 + I_2 + I_3 + I_4 = I_5$	$= I$	$5 =$	

IMPACTS ASSOCIATED WITH WORK

Scale	Items	Raw	Divided	Average
Work Productivity — Scale J	$J_1 + J_2 + J_3 + J_4 = J_5$	$= J$	$5 =$	
Work Atmosphere — Scale K	$K_1 + K_2 + K_3 = K$	$= K$	$3 =$	

IMPACTS ASSOCIATED WITH FAMILY

Household Functioning
$\square$ L1 + $\square$ L2 + $\square$ L3 = $\square$ L $\square$ ÷ 3 = $\square$

Personal Well-Being Scale M
$\square$ M1 + $\square$ M2 + $\square$ M3 + $\square$ M4 + $\square$ M5 = $\square$ M $\square$ ÷ 5 = $\square$

Family Schedules Scale N
$\square$ N1 + $\square$ N2 + $\square$ N3 + $\square$ N4 + $\square$ N5 = $\square$ N $\square$ ÷ 5 = $\square$

Family Satisfaction Scale O
$\square$ O1 + $\square$ O2 + $\square$ O3 + $\square$ O4 = $\square$ O $\square$ ÷ 4 = $\square$

Family Consensus Scale P
$\square$ P1 + $\square$ P2 + $\square$ P3 + $\square$ P4 + $\square$ P5 = $\square$ P $\square$ ÷ 5 = $\square$

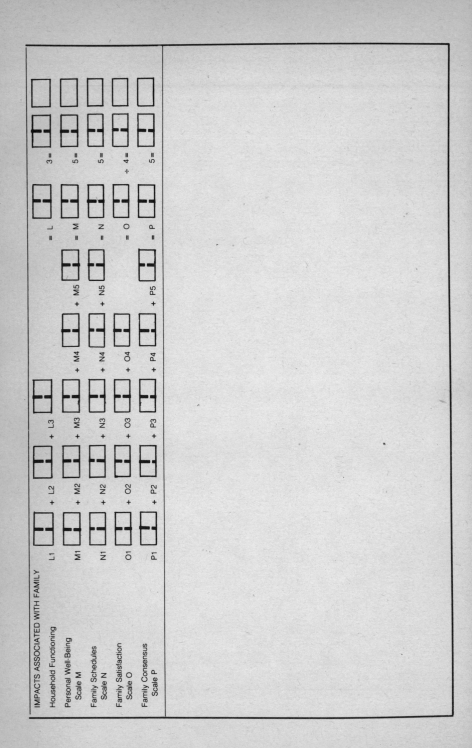